Original Sin?

SERIES EDITORS

David L. Brunsma
David G. Embrick

SERIES ADVISORY BOARD

Margaret Abraham
Elijah Anderson
Eduardo Bonilla-Silva
Philomena Essed
James Fenelon
Evelyn Nakano Glenn
Tanya Golash-Boza
David Theo Goldberg
Patricia Hill Collins
José Itzigsohn
Amanda Lewis
Michael Omi
Victor Rios
Mary Romero

Original Sin?

The Reproduction of Racism in a Multiracial Church

Willie Barnes Jr.
and
J. Scott Carter

The University of Georgia Press
ATHENS

Sociology of Race and
Ethnicity web page

© 2025 by the University of Georgia Press
Athens, Georgia 30602
www.ugapress.org
All rights reserved
Designed by Kaelin Chappell Broaddus
Set in 10.5/13.5 Garamond Premier Pro Regular
by Mary McKeon

Most University of Georgia Press titles are available from popular e-book vendors.

Printed digitally

EU Authorized Representative
Easy Access System Europe—Mustamäe tee 50,
10621 Tallinn, Estonia,
gpsr.requests@easproject.com

Library of Congress Cataloging-in-Publication Data
Names: Barnes, Willie, Jr., 1986– author | Carter, J. Scott (Sociology teacher) author
Title: Original sin? : the reproduction of racism in a multiracial church / Willie Barnes Jr. and J. Scott Carter.
Description: Athens : The University of Georgia Press, [2025] | Series: Sociology of race and ethnicity | Includes bibliographical references and index.
Identifiers: LCCN 2025003797 | ISBN 9780820374161 hardback | ISBN 9780820374178 paperback | ISBN 9780820374185 epub | ISBN 9780820374192 pdf
Subjects: LCSH: Without Walls International Church (Tampa, Fla.) | Multiethnic churches—Florida | Racism—Religious aspects—Christianity | Christian sociology | Church and social problems | United States—Race relations | United States—Religious life and customs
Classification: LCC BV625 .B375 2025 | DDC 261.809759/65—dc23 /eng/20250625

LC record available at https://lccn.loc.gov/2025003797

*To Fran Reid-Barnes and Shannon Carter,
whose support and love cannot be measured*

CONTENTS

ACKNOWLEDGMENTS IX

INTRODUCTION 1

CHAPTER 1. Context of Multiracial Churches 23

CHAPTER 2. Color-Blind Ideology and the Reproduction of Racism 45

CHAPTER 3. Social Justice, Socio-Theological Color-Blind Frames, and the Reproduction of Racism 69

CHAPTER 4. Racialized Organizations and the Reproduction of Racism 88

CHAPTER 5. Where Does All of This Fit? 109

APPENDIX 119

NOTES 125

REFERENCES 127

INDEX 143

ACKNOWLEDGMENTS

Willie Barnes Jr.: I would first like to thank my family. To my wife and partner, Fran, thank you for your support the sacrifices you made to ensure I made it to this point. Your words of encouragement and "gentle" reminders to focus made all the difference. Of course, I also want to thank Harleaux, my firstborn daughter. While I know you are more intrigued by your four-year-old activities than hearing about daddy's sociological interests, in time I hope you realize this work was fueled by you and my desire to show by example that you can accomplish anything with hard work, perseverance, and the support of your family. I also want to thank my grandmother Frances Barnes. From infancy, this strong woman raised, loved, and nurtured me. I would not be here without you! Finally, I want to thank my mentor and academic partner, Dr. J. Scott Carter. Since our first meeting, the summer before I started my PhD journey at UCF, you have advised, encouraged, and guided me through the rigors of research and scholarship. Thank you for believing in me, believing in this project, and partnering with me to reach this milestone.

J. Scott Carter: I want to first thank my family. Without their unending support and love, this book would not have been possible. First, to my wife, Shannon K. Carter, who is a top scholar in her area and professor at the University of Central Florida. She has provided me with the space over the years to ramble on about my research without complaint. I would not be here without her. Second, to my kids, who have supported me more than they can ever know. They have provided me with unending joy and energy that made this work possible. I would also like to thank others who have helped me over the years. First and foremost, I want to thank Dr. Willie Barnes Jr. for including me on this journey and teaching me a great deal about how religion and race intersect. Dr. Barnes' insights about our social world and humanistic approach to this research are unmatched and will stay with me forever. I would also like to acknowledge the great scholars I have been blessed to work with over the years, whose work is reflected in this book and who have helped me in countless ways, including Mamadi Corra, Cameron Lippard, David Embrick, David Brunsma, Eduardo Bonilla-Silva, Elijah Anderson, Micheal Hughes, Steven Tuch, Lala Steelman, and Brian Powell to name a few. Any successes I can claim are rooted in the help and guidance provided by these kind and generous scholars.

Original Sin?

INTRODUCTION

On May 25, 2020, shockwaves rippled across the United States and around the globe, as the world watched in disbelief and horror as George Floyd Jr. was murdered on video at the knee of Officer Derek Chauvin. The national and international reactions were unprecedented (Buchanan, Bui, and Patel 2020). Streets that were previously empty due to quarantines and isolation related to the deadly COVID-19 pandemic were now filled with people of every race, color, and creed risking their lives to make their voices heard in the fight against racial injustice, systemic racism, White supremacy, and police brutality.

An estimated 15 to 26 million Americans participated in these demonstrations in the weeks following Floyd's murder (Buchanan, Bui, and Patel 2020). The international response was also overwhelming, with demonstrations taking place in more than sixty countries, including Britain, France, Germany, Denmark, Italy, Syria, Brazil, Mexico, Ireland, New Zealand, Canada, Poland, and Australia (Weine et al. 2020; Rahim and Picheta 2020). Corporate America soon followed (Hessekiel 2020), showing its unprecedented support. Companies such as Nike, Ben and Jerry's, Verizon, Facebook, Amazon, Coca-Cola, and many more embarked on aggressive antiracist campaigns, pledging millions of dollars to Black organizations and causes (Hessekiel 2020). The sports world also reacted in horror to the murder. National Basketball Association (NBA) commissioner Adam Silver and players such as Lebron James expressed outrage and pledged support to end police brutality and racial injustice. The summer of 2020 witnessed the confluence of two pandemics, COVID-19 and systemic racial injustice, both exposing the structural inequalities that have riddled American institutions since the country's inception.

The viral video death of George Floyd Jr. forced many, some for the first time, to confront the legacy of institutional and structural racism in America, especially religious leaders. Many church leaders across various denominations made statements denouncing racial injustices and persistent racism and endorsing the Black Lives Matter (BLM) movement. A Barna ChurchPulse poll released on June 16, 2020, found that 94 percent of U.S. pastors agreed that the church has a responsibility to denounce racism and 76 percent said the church should support peaceful protests in response to Floyd's death (Roach 2020).

Unfortunately, many White church leaders and White Christians in general across the country either remained silent, affirmed their support of police, and/or followed the lead of President Donald Trump, who strongly advocated for "law and order" in response to the demonstrations and protests. These individuals chose to focus on the relatively few incidents of violence, rioting, and looting that accompanied the protests, rather than on the persistence of racial injustice. In describing White evangelical Christians, Andrew Manis (2020) stated, "They can be counted on yet again to renew their support of Donald Trump, enthusiastically joining the call for violent reprisal against the protestors and sticking their fingers in their ears while they intone 'Blue Lives Matter.' Or they will superficially focus on the looting and destruction of property, which by all accounts to date have not been perpetrated by protestors but by lawless elements on the extreme left and right intent on exploiting the protests under cover of nightfall."[1] This marriage between Trump and White evangelicals can also be seen in some of the responses to the clearing of protestors in the area around Lafayette Park in Washington, D.C., on June 1, 2020 (Teague 2020). These peaceful demonstrators were forcibly removed from the area so the president could take a photo, holding a Bible, outside St. John's Church. While many were flabbergasted, one evangelical supporter was quoted as saying, "He's establishing the Lord's kingdom in the world" (Teague 2020). In short, as Manis (2020) noted, Trump used the movement for Black lives as a platform from which to appeal to his base, including White conservative evangelical Christians.

Unsurprisingly, it is precisely the relationship between White evangelical Christians and Donald Trump that served as the tipping point for the exodus of many Black worshipers from White evangelical churches, as they witnessed their church leaders' endorsement of a candidate they believed blatantly trafficked in racism to appeal to his base and improve his political standing. A March 9, 2018, *New York Times* article by Campbell Robertson, titled "A Quiet Exodus: Why Black Worshipers Are Leaving White Evangelical Churches," described the experiences of Black people who turned to their religion and religious leaders for hope in the wake of the 2016 U.S. presidential election, only to be marginalized, ignored, and mistreated. According to Robertson, many felt the tension of worshiping in these spaces even prior to the controversial 2016 election of Trump to the presidency. The death of Trayvon Martin in 2012 engendered a series of protests, demonstrations, and the birth of the BLM movement in response to several high-profile deaths of unarmed Black people by law enforcement, including Eric Garner, Michael Brown Jr., Tamir Rice, Walter Scott, and Freddie Gray. These individuals became symbols of the persistence of racial injustices around the country in various places and spaces, except within many White evangelical churches. For the individuals chronicled in Robertson's article, this was just the beginning of African Americans' uneasiness in predominantly White churches as church leaders failed to address these deaths, affirm Black lives, and condemn racism.

Although members were not directly told to vote for Donald Trump, statements like the following reveal the ways in which White, evangelical pastors publicly supported Trump (Robertson 2018):

> The election," he said, "is extremely important." The country is in trouble financially; a critical Supreme Court appointment awaits; one of the major parties advocated using "taxpayer dollars, your dollars," for abortion. Evangelical Christians sit at home on Election Days, while "those who are trying to change our Constitution" go to the polls, and look at what happens: Prayer is taken out of schools. "We are going the wrong way," he concluded. "We need to get involved, we need to pray and we need to vote."

The implications of this pastor's sermon were clear: vote Christian and vote Trump. These kinds of messages and Trump's ultimate victory caused some Black parishioners to reach out to fellow congregants, many of whom were White and supported Trump. Their often cold, unconcerned, and dogmatic responses led many of those described in Robertson's article to either distance themselves or leave their churches altogether.

Although the total number of Black worshipers who left their congregations for these and other similar reasons is not known, it is clear that many were significantly impacted by the 2016 election. For example, Robertson quotes Michael Emerson, coauthor of *Divided by Faith: Evangelical Religion and the Problem of Race in America* as saying, "The election itself was the single most harmful event to the whole movement of reconciliation in at least the past 30 years." Emerson's statement reflects how the 2016 election exposed the world to the White supremacist ideology that still operates in White evangelical churches today. The silent exodus of Black Americans is a reaction to the racism these meso-level organizations produce and reproduce under the guise of Christian principles (Jones 2020).[2] The uneasiness of these Black worshipers also stems, in part, from their close proximity and location within White institutional space they must occupy every Sunday. The history of racial reconciliation, the impacts of meso-level organizational factors, and the weight of White institutional space are key factors discussed in this book.

Many of the Black worshipers interviewed by Robertson fled to kinder, multiracial, and diverse spaces, including predominantly Black churches.[3] It has been argued that such spaces are more welcoming to those of different races and ethnicities (DeYoung et al. 2003; Marti 2005, 2009; Dougherty, Marti, and Martinez 2015); however, a growing body of social science research suggests that these multiracial churches are not as progressive as one would think and are often characterized by similar challenges, especially when it comes to race and racism, as White churches (Cobb, Perry, and Dougherty 2015; Jenkins and Dillon 2012; Edwards 2008a, 2008b, 2014; Dovidio, Gaertner, and Saguy 2015; Ince 2022; Munn 2018; Oneya Okuwobi, Powell, and Ward 2020; Oyakawa 2019).

Accordingly, this book adds to a growing body of research that seeks to understand how racism and discrimination can make their way into churches where congregants from different racial and ethnic backgrounds come together for worship and fellowship. The site chosen for this study, the Without Walls Church (WWC) in South Florida, extends past the Black/White congregational context. A very racially diverse community, WWC includes Hispanic and Asian congregants as well. While some interview participants described the diversity of WWC as "a picture of how heaven will be," this is only one facet of this diverse, international congregation with thousands of members flocking to worship on Sunday mornings and engaging in outreach opportunities during the week. For many seminarians and pastors, especially those who feel led to serve in a multicultural and multiracial context, this would be a "dream" church to lead. As we sought to discover whether this community indeed lives up to the promise, our analysis focused particularly on the role of racial ideology reproduction (through framing of race, racism, and racial issues) and on policies and practices within the organization. Data for this project come from a series of interviews with church members and leaders, participant observation of church events, and content analysis of organizational media information. (Please see appendix 1 for a full description of methods and analytical strategies implemented).

Past social science research warns us that multiracial congregations may not be the liberalizing force scholars and lay people think they should be. For example, the work of Ryon Cobb and colleagues (2015) found that White members of multiracial churches were not moved by the greater diversity and held similar deleterious views about the causes of racial inequality in the United States as those from homogeneous churches. Korie L. Edwards (2008a, 2008b) similarly noted that White members at multiracial churches seemed ambivalent about race and did not seem aware of how it shaped their lives. Moreover, both Cobb and colleagues (2015) and Edwards (2008) found Black members of such congregations more likely to espouse individualistic explanations of racial inequality (e.g., lack of work ethic) while ignoring broader structural forces that produce and reproduce the racial status quo (e.g., hiring discrimination). Such findings are troubling given that one purpose of the multiracial church community is to promote interracial relationships that should foster understanding of the challenges facing Black folks and other marginalized groups (DeYoung et al. 2003).

This book has two basic goals. The first is to shed light on whether leaders and members of a specific multiracial church perpetuate a racist ideology through the use of *frames* that minimize the struggle against racism and discrimination facing Black folks and other marginalized groups in the contemporary United States, including but not limited to the four color-blind frames described by Eduardo Bonilla-Silva (2018). Bonilla-Silva posed that institutional racism (e.g., unequal treatment within the criminal justice system) is propped up by a slippery ideology that he termed color-blind racism, which appears to be less "racist" yet easily reproduces the racial status quo by dismissing persistent racial problems using seemingly nonracial explanations. Because it lacks the concreteness of Jim Crow racism, Bonilla-Silva (2018) referred to color-blind racism as racism lite, despite it being as destructive. While we explore how Bonilla-Silva's color-blind frames are used in the church, we also push past these frames and look at unique color-blind frames *specific* to theology and scripture that characterize some religious spaces. In doing so, we extend the work of Assata Zerai (2011), exploring how such frames are used by leaders and members of the wwc to minimize support for social justice activism as well.

The second goal of this work is to look at the policies and practices of wwc and assess whether they contribute to racial inequality. Work by scholars in this area pose that multiracial churches are not independent institutions disconnected from the broader socio-racial context; rather, they are deeply connected to and reflect the racial order that surrounds them (Edwards 2008a, 2018b; Priest and Priest 2007). Accordingly, it would not be surprising that such churches would bend toward the needs of White congregants and "affirm their religiocultural preferences and interests in order to sustain a racially diverse congregation" (Edwards 2008a, 5). In investigating this question, we extend the work of Victor Ray (2019), who argued that organizations are key cogs of a broader racial system because they act to constrain the agency of ethnic minorities, legitimate the unequal distribution of resources, and treat Whiteness as a credential. While some research has raised concerns over meso-level practices of multiracial churches (Edwards 2014), studies attempting to demonstrate exactly how these organizations reproduce the racial status quo at the practical level are to date limited.

Before moving forward, we would like to note that our interviews and observations occurred during a watershed moment in American history, one where Americans and individuals from around the world stood up to police brutality and racial injustices following the murder of George Floyd Jr. While unexpected, this scenario provided a rather unique opportunity to assess if and how extraordinary external forces marked by tragedy and a massive human response related to race and racial injustice can lead to challenges and, ultimately, changes to oppressive policies and processes within the WWC. Given that context matters, what impact did these events have on this church and its leaders and members? We believe such observations may provide insights into how broader forces can positively impact an organization beyond this specific case study.

The book explores the identified questions through the theoretical lens of racialized social systems theory as developed by Eduardo Bonilla-Silva (1997) (discussed in chapter 2), which poses that "in all racialized social systems the placement of people in racial categories involves some form of hierarchy that produces definite social relations between the races" (469). This hierarchy moves past just beliefs and attitudes. It has real impact on material conditions of the groups involved, with the group higher in the hierarchy receiving great socioeconomic benefits at all levels while groups lower in the hierarchy receive fewer benefits (Williams 1990; Omi and Winant 2015). Implicitly, those at the top benefit socially, materially and politically while those at the bottom suffer. This structural understanding of racial ideology can be reproduced even by non-Whites and in multiracial settings; hence, its relevance to the specific research goals in this book.[4]

In the sections that follow, we first discuss the history of religious racism in the United States and then turn our attention to the multiracial congregation that provided the data for this study.

Religious Racism in the United States.

The Reverend Dr. Martin Luther King Jr. allegedly once remarked that the most segregated hour in America was Sunday morning at 11:00 a.m., as Americans worshipped in the most segregated institution in the United States, "the Church" (Driskill, Arjannikova, and Meyer 2014; Scheitle and Dougherty 2010). Although these comments are often attributed to King, there is some evidence that the phrase most likely originated at the end of the nineteenth century as a critique of segregated churches in the northern United States (Marty 1990).

Regardless of who first articulated this idea, the sentiment seems to still ring true today. Early research findings reveal that 90 percent of congregations are 90 percent one race (Emerson and Smith 2000) and nearly 80 percent of congregations are at least 95 percent one racial group (Chaves 1998). Despite a clear growth in multiracial congregations, over 75 percent of Americans in 2018–2019 continue to attend churches where 80 percent of the congregation is made up of at least one racial group (Dougherty, Chaves, and Emerson 2020). Evidently, despite the racial integration that has been occurring in other institutions such as schools, businesses, and government and despite notable shifts in the racial makeup of congregations (toward more diversity), the vast majority of the more than three hundred thousand religious congregations in the United States—the largest and most active voluntary associations in the country—involve members who are of the same race (Emerson and Chai Kim 2018). A cursory review of America's racialized religious history provides some insights in to this uniracial composition of America's churches.

AN UNHOLY ALLIANCE

In the 1950s social scientists began to fully explore the intersection of racism and religion. Their findings suggested a counterintuitive, problematic relationship between religious ideology, racism, and prejudice. Those who held mainstream religious positions characterized by humanitarianism and equality simultaneously endorsed racist and prejudicial views (Allport 1950; Adorno et al. 1950; Jackson and Hunsberger 1999). How can one espouse Christian virtues while engaging in racialized oppression? According to some scholars, this contradiction is due to group dynamics in which identification with a religious group also promotes out-group prejudices (Burris and Jackson 2000; Jackson and Hunsberger 1999). Loyalty to one's religious group may increase the likelihood that one draws strict boundary lines with others who are outside the group. Others have found that religious racism may also stem from the same values and principles that guide the faith. These include social conventionalism, dogmatic belief structure, social conformity, and traditionalism (Hill, Matz, and Wood 2010), which when applied to a racialized context may promote racism, prejudice, and ethnocentricity.

In contrast, Robert Jones (2020, 6) argues that the cause of racism in White Christian churches is much simpler: "White Christian churches have not just been complacent; they have not only been complicit; rather, as the dominant cultural power in America, they have been responsible for constructing and sustaining a project to protect White supremacy and resist Black equality. This project has framed the entire American story. American Christianity's theological core has been thoroughly structured by an interest in protecting White supremacy." For Jones, White churches aren't just made up of racists congregants, they are the primary reproducers of racism in America. In his view, the intricate relationship between the White church and White supremacy is tied together by a theology that supports the notion of White superiority and the sanctioning of violence that preserves the racial order.

To understand institutional racism within the realm of religion, specifically Christianity, one must go back to America's founding. Long before America freed itself from British rule, the 1667 Virginia General Assembly declared that being baptized did not exempt a slave from bondage (Virginia General Assembly 1823). The purpose of this legislation was to encourage slaveowners to evangelize and convert their slaves to Christianity without having to question whether doing so changed their legal status. Some scholars pose that the framers of this law knew of the incompatibility between chattel slavery and the liberty of the Gospel. To accommodate institutionalized slavery, missionaries adapted the Christian message, emphasizing spiritual deliverance and obedience to slave overseers (Tisby 2019). Noticeably, theology was shaped in a manner allowing the spirit of slaves to be freed while denying that same freedom to their physical bodies. This theological manipulation formed the mainstream belief structure for America's White denominations.

DIFFERENT DENOMINATIONS, SAME MISSION

As time progressed, an uneasy tension developed within the nation's largest White denominations. In 1789 the Virginia Baptist General Committee declared slavery to be violent and inconsistent with American principles and called for its abolishment (Gourley 2015). After an intense outcry by enslavers, the Virginia Baptist General Committee recanted its statement and declared the topic to be outside the purview of the church. Additionally, the Southern Baptist Convention (SBC) split from Triennial Convention in 1845 when Baptist leaders decided to form an organization inclusive of slaveholders (Tisby 2019). Although some Baptist leaders attempted for some time to provide a revisionist account of the role of slavery in this separation, leading Baptist historian Leon McBeth stated unequivocally, "Slavery was the main issue that led to the 1845 schism; that is a cold historical fact" (Jones 2020, 4).

In this respect, White Methodists in the South seemed to be no different than their White Baptist counterparts. After an 1808 Methodist General Conference gave regional conferences the right to determine if their members could be slaveholders, the Methodist Church split in two in 1845, allowing clergy in the Methodist Episcopal Church, South to practice slavery (Tisby 2019). In fact, every man who ascended to the office of bishop in the Methodist Episcopal Church, South from 1846 until the Civil War owned slaves (Emerson and Smith 2000). It should be noted that while they disagreed about slavery, both Northern and Southern Methodists agreed that Black Methodists should hold a subservient position within their church structure and society (Jones 2020). Similarly, the history of the Presbyterian Church reveals a church with a deeply troubling racial past. Specifically, Presbyterians in the South formed the Presbyterian Church in the Confederate States of America, now the Presbyterian Church in the United States, and advocated for each state's right to determine its position on the legality of slavery (Tisby 2019).

The White supremacy rhetoric of prominent White Christian denominations didn't stop after the issue of slavery was resolved following the defeat of the Confederacy in the Civil War. During the Reconstruction period, newly freed Blacks made political progress, particularly in the South. Black people organized equal rights leagues, African American men were constitutionally granted citizenship and the right to vote, and over two thousand African Americans were elected to public offices across the country. To stop these advances, some Whites in the South embarked on a religiously tinged movement of resistance to the new reality. According to Jones (2020), "Mapping the experience of Civil War defeat and the resurgence of White supremacy onto Christian conceptions of crucifixion, resurrection, and salvation, they [the defeated Southerners] dubbed this new period 'Redemption'" (27). And so Whites began to violently take back political control and reassert their dominance, using methods that are fairly characterized as White Christian terrorism. This was made possible in part due to the fact that many White Christians who had advocated the abolition of slavery nevertheless continued to hold White supremacist attitudes (Emerson and Smith 2000). In the end, Whites combined racial terror with religion during the Redemption period, often leaving church on Sunday morning and participating in the lynchings, beatings, and burnings of Black Americans Sunday afternoon. Jones (2020) describes a shocking case when an African American man by the name of Samuel Thomas Wilkes was being burned alive as a White Christian man shouted, "Glory be to God." As the twentieth century approached, not only did members of White churches participate in this violence but these institutions also served as the glue of the campaign against Black equality, legitimizing and sanctioning segregation both within their walls and society more broadly.

WHITE CHURCHES AND THE CIVIL RIGHTS MOVEMENT

The 1950s and '60s were a contentious and tumultuous time in American history. During this period, many African Americans, led by clergyman, protested, marched, and demonstrated, risking their lives for the sake of equality and justice. In response, sweeping legislation was passed, expanding the scope of rights for African Americans. While Black churches were at the forefront of these movements, White churches, for the most part, withheld support and retreated to their White supremacist roots.

The 1954 landmark Supreme Court *Brown v. Topeka Board of Education* decision ruled segregation in public schools to be unconstitutional. While the leadership of the SBC affirmed this decision, local SBC churches were angered. For example, churches in Jackson, Mississippi, were complicit in the passing of a 1963 ordinance that made it an offense, punishable by law, for any African American to worship at a White church even if they were there peaceably and at the invitation of a White parishioner (Jones 2020). The split between denominational stances and local church culture was codified in a Mississippi State Legislature bill known as the "Church Property Bill," which allowed local churches to retain their property while defying their denominational policies and remaining segregated. One of the bill's authors stated its importance when he claimed, "If integration came to Mississippi, it will enter through the front door of churches" (Jones 2020, 43). This was a prospect that needed to be defended against.

As it relates to the broader movement, southern evangelicals often ignored racism and racial discrimination altogether. A review of the leading evangelical periodical *Christianity Today* from 1957–1965 found on average less than two articles per year on the topic of race (Emerson and Smith 2000). How could a publication not talk about the issue dominating headlines at the time? According to Michael Emerson and Christian Smith (2000, 46), news articles from journalists covering the civil rights movement "went unpublished for fear of giving the impression that civil rights should be part of the Christian agenda." In silencing voices in favor of civil rights, evangelicals allowed the proliferation of White supremacy. Moreover, Billy Graham, the leading and most popular evangelical voice of the twentieth century, wavered and often sided with White supremacists. In response to angry Whites who felt as though Graham was critical of segregation, Graham stated (Emerson and Smith 2000, 47), "I feel that I have been misinterpreted on racial segregation. We follow the existing social customs in whatever part of the country in which we minister. As far as I have been able to find in my study of the Bible, it has nothing to say about segregation or nonsegregation. I came to Jackson to preach only the Bible and not enter into local issues." Although Graham never permitted enforced segregation at prayer meetings he led following the *Brown v. Board of Education* decision, he was critical of the methodology of the civil rights movement (Emerson and Smith 2000). More specifically, Graham did not agree with the movement's direct-action philosophy, preferring instead a gradual approach.

Emerson and Smith (2000) argue that this combination of minimizing racism and condemning civil rights activism were rooted in White supremacist theology. Evangelicals of this period believed that the world would continuously decline morally until Christ returned. To dedicate oneself to causes furthering social justice was pointless because the world was going to only become worse, no matter what one did. This combination of Christian nihilism and racism protected the racial order and allowed for the uninterrupted reproduction of White supremacy. At the same time, although most local White churches were against civil rights, the denominational statements supporting civil rights foreshadowed the reconciliation movements to come.

RACIAL RECONCILIATION

In the wake of the civil rights movement, a theology of racial reconciliation developed among both Black and White church leaders. According to Emerson and Smith (2000), this was sparked by the coming of age of three Black men in the late 1960s who became known as the founding fathers of reconciliation. John Perkins, Tom Skinner, and Samuel Hines all desired to see the end of racial divisions in the United States and felt reconciliation was at the heart of the Christian message. Accordingly, they developed a theology of reconciliation based on Ephesians 2:14–15 (NKJV): "For He Himself is our peace, who has made both one, and has broken down the middle wall of separation, having abolished in His flesh the enmity, that is, the law of commandments contained in ordinances, so as to create in Himself one new man from the two, thus making peace." Based on these views and other Scripture, they believed the goal of Christianity was to demonstrate God's power through the work of reconciliation.

Based on the work of these early leaders, George Yancey, an eminent professor of the social sciences at Baylor University, outlined four steps to achieve racial reconciliation (Emerson and Smith 2000). These include (1) the development of primary relationships across races; (2) the recognition of the social structures of inequality and the coming together of Christians to resist those structures; (3) the repentance by Whites of their "personal, historical, and social sins"; and (4) the extension of forgiveness on the part of Blacks toward Whites. And indeed, some steps were taken in this direction, by Billy Graham in particular. For example, a 1965 headline in *Christianity Today* read, "Billy Graham in Montgomery: A Stride Toward Reconciliation" (Emerson and Smith 2000, 56). At this point in Graham's ministry, he involved Black Americans in nearly every facet of his meetings, including prayers and music.

Decades later, the reconciliation movement began to formally take shape with the proliferation of books, organizations, and formal apologies (Emerson and Smith 2000). Texts such as Spencer Perkins and Chris Rice's *More than Equals: Racial Healing for the Sake of the Gospel*, John Perkins and Thomas Tarrants' *He's My Brother: Former Racial Foes Offer Strategies for Reconciliation*, and Tony Evans' *Let's Get to Know Each Other* flooded the market and became study texts for congregations around the country. Furthermore, in 1994 the Pentecostal Fellowship of North America dissolved its organization in an effort to seek reconciliation with Black Pentecostal denominations, forming the Pentecostal/Charismatic Churches of North America (Emerson and Smith 2000). The following year, the SBC apologized for its involvement in slavery. While commemorating the 150th anniversary of its founding, the SBC passed a formal resolution that "repudiated 'historic acts of evil such as slavery from which we continue to reap a bitter harvest. They also acknowledged that SBC churches 'failed, in many cases, to support, and in some cases opposed, legitimate initiatives to secure the civil rights of African-Americans' and issued an apology 'to all African-Americans for condoning and/or perpetuating individual and systemic racism in our lifetime" (Jones 2020, 54). Other organizations also made it their mission to focus on racial reconciliation, including InterVarsity Christian Fellowship, Harambee Center, the Twin Cities Urban Reconciliation Network, Urban Reconciliation Enterprise, the John M. Perkins Foundation for Reconciliation and Development, and Promise Keepers.

While these organizations and other denominations made headlines for their statements of reconciliation, they were also criticized by many. The main critique of the reconciliation movement was that it ignored the consequences of systemic, structural, and institutional racism for Black Americans. Its adherents also failed to commit through ongoing actions to practical and tangible reparations for the historic legacy of White supremacy. And in the end, challenges to racial reconciliation proliferated, including the Southern Strategy, the rise of Ronald Reagan, and the anti-affirmative action measures of the Bush 43 administration (Inwood 2015; Tonry 1995; Awad, Cokley, Ravitch 2005), culminating in the political ascendancy of Donald Trump, which definitively brought the movement to an end.

THE RISE OF WHITE CHRISTIAN NATIONALISM

Donald Trump's ethnic and religious trolling of former president Barack Obama typified the rise of what many have come to refer as White Christian nationalism.

For example, in 2011, Trump made the following unsubstantiated comment in a Fox News interview (Jones 2020, 13): "He doesn't have a birth certificate. He may have one, but there's something on that, maybe religion, maybe it says he is a Muslim." Later, after Trump threw himself into the political arena, a Trump supporter remarked at a rally in New Hampshire, "'We have a problem in this country. It's called Muslims. You know our current president is one. You know he's not even an American.' Chuckling, Trump replied, 'We need this question. This is the first question'" (Jones 2020, 13).

Appealing to anti-ethnic and anti-Muslim sentiments, Trump was speaking directly to the heart of White Christian nationalists. It proved to be a winning strategy. According to election polls and postelection analysis, Trump received 81 percent of the White evangelical protestant vote, 64 percent of the White Catholic vote, and 57 percent of the White mainline Protestant vote (Jones 2020, 15). Deploying his own racism, Trump was able to solidify this White Christian base through appeals to White supremacy. Jones (2020, 15) notes that "Trump's powerful appeal to White evangelicals was not that he spoke to the culture wars around abortion or same-sex marriage, or his populist appeals to economic anxieties, but rather that he evoked powerful fears about the loss of White Christian dominance amid a rapidly changing environment." Indeed, although White clergy, as mentioned previously, stood for moral principles such as opposition to abortion, it was really the defense of the racial order that prompted White Christians to support Trump.

This development was exemplified in Trump's response and White clergy's reaction to the horrors that took place in Charlottesville, Virginia, in August 2017 as a group of White nationalists, neo-Nazis, and neo-Confederates clashed with counterprotesters at the Unite the Right rally held to protest the removal of a statue of Confederate general Robert E. Lee. The clash resulted in the death of one woman. In the wake of this tragedy, President Trump remarked there was "blame on both sides" and that there were "very fine people on both sides." Amid the national outcry over the president's comments, prominent White evangelical leaders such as Jerry Falwell Jr., Franklin Graham, Robert Jeffress, and Tony Perkins explicitly approved of Trump's comments, going as far as to blame the victims for the riots and refusing to condemn racism (Balmer 2017; Boston 2017). A union that could only mirror the one between White slaveholding Christians in the South and the Confederacy in the nineteenth century had now taken place in the twenty-first century between the White House and the leaders of "God's" house.

Gorski (2009, 91) defines Christian nationalism as a "blending of Christian and patriotic narratives and iconography that blurs or erases the line between religious and political community and identity." Utilizing narratives, traditions, myths, value systems, and symbols, Christian nationalism articulates the idea that America is "Christian" and that this fact should be expressed in the public square through policies, symbols, and other manifestations of overall national identity (Baker, Perry, and Whitehead 2020). Further, White Christian nationalism venerates America's past (e.g., founding fathers, documents, ideals, etc.) and emphasizes the need for the country to go back to its Christian foundation (Davis and Perry 2020). In response to demographic and cultural fears, Whites can use religious language to mask Christian nationalism's true exclusionary and authoritarian nature.

Numerous studies have explored the implications of the White Christian nationalist ideological framework. This research suggests that White Christian nationalists are more likely than other groups to draw rigid racial boundaries around national group membership, limit civil liberties of "out-groups," and hold prejudicial attitudes toward Blacks and other minorities (Carter and Carter 2014; Carter and Carter 2017; Carter and Corra 2005; Carter and Corra 2012; Carter and Corra 2016; Carter et al. 2014; Carter, Corra, and Jenks 2016; Carter and Lippard 2020; Carter et al. 2005; Embrick, Carter, and Lippard 2020; Perry and Whitehead 2015a; Perry, Whitehead, and Davis 2019); support the death penalty (Davis 2018; Dotson and Carter 2012); support policies expanding religion's role in government, discouraging debt, and enforcing biblical morality and work ethic (Aho 2013; Goldberg 2006); tolerate racists politically (Davis and Dovidi 2020); oppose interracial marriage and families (Perry and Whitehead 2015a, 2015b); deny the existence of police brutality toward Blacks (Perry, Whitehead, and Davis 2019); hold negative attitudes toward immigrants (Sherkat and Lehman 2018) and religious minorities, including Muslims (Dahab and Omori 2019; Shortle and Gaddie 2015; Stewart, Edgell, and Delehanty 2018; Edgell and Tranby 2010; Merino 2010; Sherkat and Lehman 2018); oppose gun control (Whitehead, Schnabel, and Perry 2018); support gender traditionalism (Whitehead and Perry 2019); demonstrate skepticism toward science and medicine (Corra and Carter 2008); be more favorable to those who engage in old-fashion racism (Davis and Perry 2020); and hold negative attitudes toward sexual minorities (Whitehead and Perry 2015). The existing literature also demonstrates that White Christian nationalists tend to oppose policies meant to alleviate racial inequality, including welfare aid and race-based affirmative action policies (Aho 2013; Goldberg 2006). In short, the implications of White Christian nationalism, politically, culturally, socially, economically, religiously, and sexually are vast, touching every facet of society, government, and culture in the United States.

Perhaps most obviously, the impact of this ideology can be seen in the role of White Christian nationalists in the election of Donald J. Trump as president in 2016. Identification with White Christian nationalism is one of the strongest predictors of animosity toward immigrants (McDaniel, Nooruddin, and Shortle 2011; Sherkat and Lehman 2018) and Muslims (Shortle and Gaddie 2015)—each a powerful predictor of support for Trump (Baker, Perry, and Whitehead 2020). According to other research, this aversion toward immigrants and Muslims can be expanded to animosity toward ethnoreligious minorities in general, including Black Americans (Ekins 2017; Major, Blodorn, and Blascovich 2018; Schaffner, MacWilliams, and Nteta 2018; Stewart 2018).

These findings suggest that there is a significant relationship between the prejudicial and exclusivist nature of White Christian nationalism and support for Trump's authoritarian personality and policies (Braunstein 2017; Gorski 2017a). Indeed, Trump has often appealed to Christian nationalists through "law and order" rhetoric, particularly in the context of the 2020 movement for Black lives. Unfortunately, this emphasis on "law and order" also includes violent and coercive methods to maintain social control over non-Whites. Although other presidents in the past, including George W. Bush, received support from White Christian nationalists, the support Donald Trump has received is unprecedented (Miller 2021).

As White Christian nationalism represents the intersection of White supremacy and religion, it is perhaps not surprising that it is pervasive in White-majority churches across the denominational spectrum. However, what is not clear is the extent of its foothold in multiracial spaces and among people of color in the Trump era. To fill this gap in our knowledge, this book seeks to understand if (and if so, how) Whiteness, White institutional space, and White supremist ideology in general may be reproduced in multiracial church settings.

In so doing, this book examines how persistent racism and racialized events are framed in the congregational space, particularly events that speak to the core of White Christian nationalism such as the 2016 election, the Charlottesville Unite the Right Rally, Colin Kaepernick's NFL protests, and the death of George Floyd Jr. While we believe that these discussions/frames shed light on how such multiracial spaces reproduce racism, we also believe that such discussions/frames can lead to the proliferation of counterframes that seek to make change at the macro (society) and meso (organization) levels. Finally, it is important to understand whether a multiracial church can be considered a racialized organization that utilizes policies and practices that produce and reproduce the racial status quo. Important to this organizational assessment is the role played by diversity initiatives and tropes that mask significant reproduction of racialization processes. We discuss these in more detail as we move forward in the book. For now, we will further examine the characteristics and significance of multiracial churches within the American religious landscape.

Multiracial Congregations

Research demonstrates that multiracial churches are becoming more prevalent in America. The proportion of multiracial churches in America nearly doubled between 1998 and 2012, accounting for 8 percent of all U.S. Christian religious communities (Emerson and Smith 2000). Even as the racial divide seems to have grown in America, the church appears to be one segment of American culture in which people are crossing racial lines. Today, some argue that multiracial congregations are the fastest growing type of large Christian churches in the United States (Yancey 2003). According to Michael Emerson (2010), large Protestant churches that consists of more than one thousand regular attendees are more than twice as likely to be multiracial now compared to a decade ago.

The term "multiracial" describes congregations that regularly hold at least one major worship service in which no racial group comprises more than 80 percent of the worshipers (Emerson and Yancey 2008; Chaves et al. 1999; Dougherty, Johnson, and Polson 2007; Dougherty, Marti, and Martinez 2015; Pitt 2010; Emerson 2006; Emerson and Chai Kim 2018; Kanter 1977; Pettigrew and Martin 1986). Race and gender studies suggest that 20 percent constitutes the point of critical mass (Emerson and Chai Kim 2018) because the proportion is high enough for the minority presence to be felt and filtered throughout a system or organization (Kanter 1977; Pettigrew and Martin 1986).

The rise in popularity of multiracial congregations could be a result of such institutions being seen as venues that could help reduce racial divisions in society (DeYoung et al. 2003). Others have noted that multiracial congregations help individuals transcend racial and ethnic differences (Marti 2005, 2009). Furthermore, the increased popularity of multiracial congregations could be attributed to other factors. Diverse congregations may inherently appeal to a wider pool of potential participants. Additionally, they allow for the inclusion of second- and third-generation immigrants who feel less connected to the ancestral cultures of their parents and grandparents than to a generalized American mainstream culture (Dougherty et al. 2015).

Scholars have also argued that the interracial contact experienced in interracial/multiracial churches sufficiently meet the conditions prescribed by Allport's (1954) contact hypothesis, which would ultimately improve race relations and reduce social distance between groups. In this vision, greater contact would foster more progressive attitudes on a variety of social issues (Johnson and Jacobson 2005; Yancey 1999, 2001, 2006). Furthermore, interracial contact within religious settings has been more consistently linked with a reduction in racial prejudice and social distance than in most other contexts (Emerson 2006; Irving 1973; Johnson and Jacobson 2005; Leacock, Deutsch, and Fishman 1959; Parker 1968; Yancey 1999, 2001, 2006).

Still, while there are opportunities for progressive and inclusive racial ideologies to develop in these settings, there continue to be issues facing these churches. As will be further discussed in chapter 1, multiracial churches tend to create racialized hierarchies that favor the interests of Whites (Jenkins and Dillon 2012, Priest and Priest 2007). These hierarchies tend to restrict racial minority groups from leadership and other positions of influence (Christerson, Edwards, and Emerson 2005; Christerson and Emerson 2003; Edwards 2008b; Emerson and Smith 2000). Research has also found that multiracial churches maintain White socioreligious norms by minimizing diverse worship practices (Jenkins and Dillon 2012) and failing to recognize systemic racial inequality and the efforts seeking to combat those inequalities (Dovidio, Gaertner, and Saguy 2015). Moreover, studies have shown multiracial congregations engage in a practice known as "ethnic transcendence," that minimizes distinct ethnic identities and promotes a congregational culture with White popular norms at its core (Garces-Foley 2007b). Finally, Zerai (2011) and Oyakawa (2019) connect the usage of colorblindness, the subordination of race-talk, and the nonpursuit of social justice in multiracial churches.

As should be clear by now, previous research on multiracial congregations presents an ambiguous picture as to whether or not they are progressive or closer in nature to their White church counterparts. While our work builds on these studies, we examine areas this previous research has largely neglected. Specifically, we will examine the potential usage of color-blind frames and minimization of counterframes and explore organizational processes that may reproduce racism as well as external events that challenge those processes. We posit that it is through extraordinary external events that change may finally come.

WITHOUT WALLS CHURCH: REFLECTIONS FROM THE FIRST AUTHOR

At 6:15 a.m. on a Sunday morning, I am anxiously making my way to the southwest location of WWC. As I am driving, I notice the Spanish style clay tile roofs that sit atop the streets' multimillion-dollar homes with large iron gates. Well-manicured lawns and palm trees speak to the attention to aesthetic detail that often accompanies wealthy communities. There is no one on the streets aside for an occasional early morning jogger and pet owner walking their dog. As I stop at red lights, I take a moment to examine the environment—the cars in driveways, the absence of the homeless, the lack of trash and litter, the quietness and solitude, and the castle-like appearance of the community's private schools.

According to the U.S. Census, this community identifies as 60 percent Hispanic or Latino and 33 percent White (non-Hispanic or Latino). These proportions represent a significantly higher than national average Hispanic/Latinx population (approximately 3 times) and a significantly lower than the national average White population (almost half).[5] Additionally, 39.5 percent of the city's population identifies as foreign born, in contrast to 13.6 percent of the U.S. population. The education, housing, and income statistics are also quite revealing. Of the population twenty-five years and older, 66.7 percent holds a bachelor's degree or higher, compared to 32.1 percent of the U.S. population. The median value of owner-occupied housing units is $846,100, compared to a U.S. average of $217,500. Lastly, the median household income is $100,843 compared to a national average of $62,843. These data reveal that the WWC is located in an atypically ethnically diverse, educated, and affluent community.

The streets in which the WWC is situated, like those of the surrounding community, are emptied. The shops are closed, and the only open business is the Starbucks located next door to the church. Pre-COVID-19, these same streets overflowed with shoppers and diners flooding to upscale restaurants, juice bars, business offices, jewelry stores, fine clothing retailers, and foreign car dealerships. Both young and old alike gathered at sidewalk seats to socialize, close business deals, enjoy the weather, and take in the sights and sounds of the community.

In this buzzing neighborhood stands the Dream Theater, the physical home of WWC. The art deco style of the building combines with its red exterior and brick pavement sidewalk in a way that transports visitors back to the days of its grand opening in 1948. The large signage on the front top of the building advertises the current production while a ticket booth sits below. Upon entering, the glossy wooden walls and floral carpets lead visitors through the double doors to the performance center, a nine-hundred-seat auditorium. It is this historic space that gives birth every Sunday to a contemporary and diverse multiracial church.

As my drive concludes, I realize I have arrived earlier than I anticipated. 6:30 a.m. is the church's set up time, as it prepares to host three services in this historic theater. In jeans and a T-shirt, I walk over to the Starbucks to kill some time and grab a coffee. As I leave the Starbucks and walk toward the back doors of the theater, the campus pastor, Hans also arrives.[6] Before this morning, we had met twice. The first time was when I first visited the church. The second meeting occurred at another Starbucks location. During this second meeting, I articulated my research interests and we discussed each other's background. Once the church's leadership

Introduction

approved my research request, he invited me to join the staff and volunteers for 6:30 a.m. setup.

As I walk in the back door, the praise team has already begun practicing with the sound engineers while thirteen to fifteen people, all seemingly under the age of forty, are busy setting up the lighting and musical equipment on stage and placing curtains and stanchions in the auditorium. In the lobby area, volunteers are setting up the welcome center and the kids' area. As I begin to interact with the staff and volunteers, I am immediately struck by their racial diversity. Blacks, Whites, Latinx, and Asians all work together under the banner of WWC. As worshipers begin to pour into the theater lobby drinking coffee, wearing shorts and T-shirts, and dropping of their children at the kids' area, I begin to realize that the racial diversity of the staff and volunteers is a mirror of the diversity among worshipers. It is clear that this is a truly multiracial space, one indicative of a multiracial and multisite church that genuinely values diversity.

As worshipers make their way into the darkened theater, the only lighting is coming from the uplighting on the stage. They are greeted by the sounds of keyboards, drums, and acoustic guitars, as the melodic voices of the praise team leads the congregation in the leading contemporary Christian music of the time. For the worshipers, there is no sitting. Across the auditorium, people are on their feet, many with their hands raised toward the heavens, singing along with the praise team and swaying back and forth. The rainbow of colors represented by these raised hands may only be matched by the multicolored lighting. After praise and worship, the campus pastor, Hans, prays, welcomes everyone, and gives a few short announcements. After another musical presentation, the screen in the auditorium comes down and instantaneously we join all the other campuses around south Florida in watching the sermon, streaming from the main location. Today, an African American preacher from Kentucky by the name of Matthew Croskey offers the sermon. Although he serves as a pastor in Kentucky, Pastor Matthew is considered a teaching pastor at WWC and regularly flies to south Florida to preach. After the sermon, Hans gives instructions about "next steps" and the offering and the worshipers are dismissed to socialize, enjoy coffee, and retrieve their children. Like a fine-tuned machine, this routine is mastered three times each Sunday. Following the last service, everything set up at 6:30 a.m. is broken down and placed upstairs, and the theater is set for the evening production.

WITHOUT WALLS CHURCH: BACKGROUND

Founded in the early 1900s, WWC claims over thirty-six thousand members (adults and children), with seven congregations in the south Florida area and international campuses in Cuba, Guatemala, Costa Rica, and Colombia. This church is also "aligned doctrinally and cooperatively in missions with the SBC." As articulated earlier, it is important to note that historically, most of the members of the SBC upheld racial segregation and rejected the aims and purposes of the civil rights movement. Still, today, the majority of SBC leaders reject the explicit racism of the past and condemn those who stood for segregation (Manis 1999).

At one time, WWC's homepage would greet each visitor with the following words: "We're a multi-cultural church that seeks to make fully devoted followers of Christ." Currently, the website describes the church as "multi-generational" and "multi-cultural." The church also claims to have members from seventy different nationalities and purports to be not only a multicultural church but an international one, a theme constantly repeated across the website and supplemental literature. This multiracial frame can also be seen in the proliferation of images of diverse people on the church's website and social media, interacting, serving, and worshipping together.

At the time this research was conceived, the lead pastor of WWC was Samuel Ashton, a White male in his sixties who held this position for more than twenty years. In October 2016, it was disclosed that "Pastor Sam" was diagnosed with cancer. The church provided updates regarding his surgery, chemotherapy, and recovery process via the church's website. The last update was posted on Sunday, October 1, 2017: "Pastor Sam's colon is cancer free! We praise God from whom all blessings flow." Pastor Sam has since stepped down from the role of lead pastor and transitioned into the role of teaching pastor. This made way for the new lead pastor, Pastor Sherman Rowen, a Turkish/Hispanic lawyer with over ten years of experience at WWC, who served as a small group leader, campus pastor, and director of campuses before assuming the new role.

WWC is overseen by the Administrative Leadership Team (ALT), which includes the lead pastor, teaching pastor, chief of staff, director of ministries, director of operations, director of campuses, and the weekend experience director. Furthermore, each location is overseen by a campus pastor. Although the campus pastors are not responsible for preaching, they do oversee their own staff. Each campus also has a full-time worship director, kids' director, and student director. There are also countless volunteers responsible for other aspects of the campus, including security, next steps, greeting, production, and so on.

Exploring the relationship between leaders and their ability to influence staff, volunteers, and members is essential to understanding how racial ideology is reproduced in organizations. Lunenburg (2012) highlights the power leaders have in influencing the people they lead. Not only can leaders influence, they also set policies and procedures and have the authority to make statements on behalf of the organization. It is also leadership that sets the boundaries for conversation and the implementation of actions resulting from those conversations. As such, the influence of leadership in the reproduction of racism in multiracial churches will also be explored in this research.

Conclusion

Over the course of U.S. history, White Christian churches have supported the rights of slaveholders and the ideology of Black inferiority, propagated White supremacy, sanctioned violence against African Americans, affirmed Jim Crow, moderated in their positions during the civil rights movement, and held conflicting stances on the movement for Black lives. This account of religious institutional racism is admittedly broad. It does not reflect the work of White abolitionists who used orthodox Christian theology as a tool to fight for the liberation of slaves and the achievement of their social equality, nor does it deal with the statements denouncing racism many White denominations issued over the course of American history even as some Northern churches espoused racism just as much as their Southern counterparts. It also does not provide an account of White church involvement in the movements for Black lives. It does reflect, however, the overwhelming evidence supporting the argument that most White churches in America have been the primary locus for the propagation and reproduction of racism and White supremacy in the United States (Jones 2020). For many, these historical and contemporary accounts of religious based oppression and White supremacy in this country are a foregone conclusion.

This book seeks to understand and explore how multiracial churches may or may not contribute to the reproduction of racialized ideologies, policies, and institutional practices akin to their White church counterparts. Wendy Leo Moore (2008, 172) states that "the social science community must continually scrutinize the contemporary operation of racial reproduction, or else we run the risk of merely producing better frameworks for understanding our past, which will have little application in the present. This means that as scholars, we must examine both the structural attributes of White racial supremacy and the discursive mechanisms and frames that constrain the ways in which we analyze and respond to structural inequality."

This is particularly relevant to this book in that Whiteness can dominate spaces even when the majority present are not White (Bonilla-Silva 2018). Overall, we seek to understand if and how in diverse religious settings, supporters of White supremacy may still promulgate racial ideology in ways similar to what happens in White spaces that maintain practices that do not benefit people of color.

Chapter 1 presents a comprehensive literature review exploring the characteristics of multiracial churches and diving deeper into the role multiracial churches play when it comes to the perpetuation of racial inequalities. Furthermore, the chapter explores White institutional space, White racial ideology, White racial identity, and honorary Whiteness and how these elements of White supremacy can be reproduced in non–majority White spaces.

In chapter 2 we discuss our data and explore the concepts of racial ideology, particularly color-blind ideology and its implications for the church in particular and for the racial structure in general. As already indicated, this ideology includes the use of color-blind frames and styles as described by Bonilla-Silva (2018) that may reproduce racism in seemingly innocuous ways. We focus specifically on how church leaders, volunteers, and members may or may not use these frames and styles.

Chapter 3 extends the work of Assata Zerai (2011) by developing new sociotheological color-blind frames and counterframes from our conversations with leaders and members of WWC. These frames not only seek to reproduce color-blind racial ideology but also minimize social justice as a counter frame by borrowing ideas from theology and Scripture.

Chapter 4 analyzes Ray's (2019) work on racialized organizations and examines how WWC may connect racial ideology to social and material resources through schemas, or taken for-granted representations, and the use of diversity themes to mask these processes. Moreover, Ray identifies social movements as sources of change for these organizations; therefore, attention will be given to how the murder of George Floyd Jr. and the social movements birthed in the aftermath of his death may or may not provide the foundation for change within WWC.

Chapter 5, the conclusion, summarizes the findings and explores potential areas of future scholastic inquiry.

CHAPTER 1

Context of Multiracial Churches

Reflections from the First Author

Somewhere around sixth grade, I began to feel the weight of "diversity." Year after year until I graduated from high school, I would enter classrooms, participate in extracurricular activities, and be elected to leadership positions. Often, I was the only Black person in these spaces. I was publicly spotlighted in ways that recognized my presence while my private conversations with my peers reminded me of my racial identity. Comments like "you speak really well for a Black person" or "you don't dress like the other Black guys" placed me in situations where I didn't know whether I was being complimented or insulted. Looking around the room, there was no one who shared my experiences, no one I could confide in. It was lonely, isolating, and tough. On the one hand, I was excited to soar academically and in other areas; on the other, I truly desired to be in spaces that were affirming and more diverse.

As I reflect on those years and the years since then, I realize there is a weight that comes with diversity, a weight that Black people, the marginalized, and people of color must bear by just entering a room. This weight includes my experiences of loneliness and isolation, but it also includes feeling as if your opinions and perspectives are discounted or you're undeserving of being in a particular space. We must help everyone bear the weight of diversity by creating spaces characterized by intentional listening, dialogue, value sharing, and equity. It is through true intentionality that these White spaces can become more equitable, just, and kind. Many people who share experiences similar to mine desire to be in community with others from different racial, ethnic, and class backgrounds. Multiracial churches have the power to provide that community; however, as we will see throughout this chapter, that power can also be used to reflect and protect the existing social order.

Introduction

The homogenous unit principle, proposed by Donald McGavran in the 1970s, argues that homogenous churches are more amenable to church growth (Wagner 1979) because members of the community do not have to contend with challenges related to differing racial, political, and cultural ideologies. Although it can be argued that this principle is less relevant today because of the rise of multiracial congregations in the United States, most congregations are still homogenous (Dougherty, Chaves, and Emerson 2020; Dougherty and Huyser 2008; Emerson 2006). Indeed, even today, it is estimated that 76 percent of Americans attend churches where one racial group comprises more than 80 percent of the congregation (Dougherty, Chaves, and Emerson 2020).

The implications of homogeneity are significant. In a case analysis of multiethnic churches, Christerson, Edwards, and Emerson (2005) found that homogenous churches represent a lost opportunity to enhance racial understandings in the church and community. Homogenous churches have also been found to develop cultural boundaries that define who is and is not like "us" (Perry 2013), which impacts community diversity. For instance, Driskill, Arjannikova, and Meyer (2014) found that stronger in-group ties correlate with reduced community diversity, while Blanchard (2007) found that segregated churches are directly related to segregated communities across all regions in the United States.

The vast ideological and theological frameworks that form the foundation for predominantly White homogenous churches create spaces in which Whiteness is celebrated and otherness is marginalized. This can be seen in the White churches' support of slavery and opposition to civil rights (Edwards 2008a, 2008b). At the same time, multiracial churches can be seen as an attempt to reject these frameworks by intentionally creating a community of diverse people. The purpose of this chapter is to examine multiracial church scholarship, White institutional space, White racial ideology, White racial identity, and honorary Whiteness to understand how these elements influence physical and social spaces, including multiracial churches, leading to the reproduction of racism.

Multiracial Churches

HISTORICAL OVERVIEW

Multiracial congregations are not a new phenomenon: they have existed ever since slaves were brought to American shores. As historian John Boles (1988, 2) writes, Blacks and Whites worshiped together, "heard the same sermon, were baptized into communion together, and upon death were buried in the same cemeteries." Emerging out of the camp meetings of the religious and social movement known as the Great Awakening of the 1740s, these biracial congregations were notable for interracial contact and the message of equality for all people (Emerson and Yancey 2008).

In these congregations, it was not uncommon for African Americans to serve in leadership roles. As historian Nathan Hatch (1989) describes, well into the 1700s, Blacks regularly preached in these racially mixed congregations and indeed Black pastors led some of them. Eventually, as alluded to earlier, American Protestantism began to succumb to segregation. Blacks were put into separate galleries, such as back pews, balconies, or were forced to stand at the back or even outside looking in through windows or open doorways (Emerson and Yancey 2008). This kind of treatment eventually led to the creation of separate Black denominations and congregations, such as the African Methodist Episcopal Church in the late 1700s.

Still, contrary to the trend of church segregation after the Civil War, interracial churches persisted. In the early 1880s, a movement emerged in the Midwest that would serve as a forerunner to the Church of God. Known as the Evening Light Saints or the Church of God Movement, this interracial movement preached a message of holiness and unity (DeYoung et. al 2003). Later, 1906 saw the eruption of the Azusa Street Revival, which lasted for about three years (DeYoung et al. 2003; Garces-Foley 2007a). Though short-lived, this movement emphasized holiness and gave birth to major Pentecostal denominations, including the Church of God in Christ and the Assemblies of God, which are still thriving today (Blumhofer 2006). Other multiracial church organizations developed in the 1920s, '30s, '40s, and '60s. Still, although multiracial congregations have long been fixtures within the religious landscape of America, uniracial or homogeneous churches have always predominated.

UNIRACIAL CHURCHES AND IDENTITY

Unsurprisingly within this historical context, homogeneity is dominant within the African American church tradition. Nearly 80 percent of African Americans who attend religious services attend congregations in Black denominations, and more than 80 percent attend congregations that are primarily Black (Lincoln and Mamiya 1990). This pattern seems to persist even today: as of 2018–2019, Black Protestants continue to attend homogeneous Black churches (Dougherty, Chaves, and Emerson 2020). Historically, the Black church served as a "haven in a heartless" world where members could congregate despite their rejection by the larger culture (Emerson 2006, 16). Described by W. E. B. Du Bois (1903, 207–208) as the "most powerful agency in the moral development and social reform of 9,000,0000 Americans of Negro blood," the Black church has been at the front lines of the fight for civil rights while also cultivating a unique ethnic and cultural identity.

Given that Black churches were founded in protest against the inequitable treatment of African Americans by Whites of the same religious faith, they became the manifestation of both Black independence and rebellion (Peart 2000). In fact, DeYoung et al. (2003, 111) cite unique features of the Black church experience, both in collective worship and in political activism, that are "not easily duplicated within multiracial congregations." At the same time, though perhaps less obviously, other research suggests that multiracial churches can also celebrate ethnic identity and respond in meaningful and productive ways to racial injustices (Driskill, Arjannikova, and Meyer 2014). Marti (2010, 212), in his study of Black identity in a multiethnic church, found that "both ethnic transcendence and ethnic reinforcement" are possible in such environments. Multiracial churches can cultivate an identity that subsumes other identities and reinforces an individual's ethnic identity in the same space. Nonetheless, a decision to seek out diversity versus staying in a Black church represents a dilemma for many Black Americans (Driscoll, Arjannikova, and Meyer 2014; Robertson 2018) as described in the *New York Times* article by Robertson discussed in the introductory chapter.

The idea of identity is prevalent in multiracial church literature, highlighting some of the challenges facing these churches. Studies show that ethnically specific identities may be subsumed within a congregationally specific identity constructed around value-rational ideals. This can cause members of diverse congregations to experience inconvenience, discomfort, and outright conflict in their cross-ethnic interactions (Dougherty and Huyser 2008; Garces-Foley 2007a, 2007b; Marti 2005). Other studies present seemingly contradictory results, finding that congregants retain particularistic ethnic designations while embracing a broader Christian identity that crosses racial lines (Alumkal 2001, 2005; Emerson 2006; Jeung 2004; Kim 2004, 2006). These conflicting findings suggest that multiracial churches are difficult to sustain as they seek to uplift different ethnic identities while creating a specific church culture and identity (Marti 2009).

The complexity of identity in these multiracial settings stems from how people assign ethnic categories to others. Social actors continually choose whether to assert, alter, or obscure their ethnic identity (Dhingra 2007; Hutchinson, Rodriguez, and Hagan 1996; Rondilla and Spickard 2007; Young 2007). Because there is often a tension between ethnic identity and multiracial church identity, there is a tremendous possibility that broader racial issues or even those specific to the congregation for that matter may go unaddressed as church leaders seek to cultivate a specific church identity (Edwards 2008a, 2008b). Highlighting racial injustices may disrupt the formation of that overall church identity, as doing so sheds light on the plight of some groups while holding others accountable for the perpetuation of racism. Edwards (2008b) and others have noted that the dominant racial order may unintentionally impact multiracial settings for all members, regardless of race. For example, leaders and members may pacify White members to maintain and grow membership. In fact, Edwards (2008a, 2008b) noted that White religious capital was an important attribute to have for pastors of multiracial churches.

CHARACTERISTICS

Existing scholarship has identified various types of multiracial churches in the United States. For example, there are clear differences between multiracial churches in the Northeast or West Coast and the Midwest and South (Dougherty and Huyser 2008; Dougherty 2003). Many multiracial churches tend to be Catholic rather than Protestant; formed as a separate entity with a focus on race relations within the context of a larger denomination; characterized by charismatic worship (applause, dancing, raised hands, speaking in "tongues"); and led by racially mixed church leadership. They are furthermore characterized by small group ministries, which seek to build intimate communities among church members, younger average membership age, newer churches, higher average congregational education and income levels, more race-related programming, and greater interpersonal interactions among congregants than other churches (Dougherty and Huyser 2008).

We also know that the primary impetus for a congregation becoming multiracial comes from its mission and resource calculation, which may reflect changes in the congregation's resource levels (Emerson and Chai Kim 2018). Efforts toward a multiracial membership to be successful depend on the availability of a racially diverse population that may be inspired to join the congregation. These new members may be drawn to the congregation for several reasons, including proximity, appeal of the congregation's culture and purpose, and preexisting organizational packages (Emerson and Chai Kim 2018).

The primary impetus for change and the source of diversification combine to produce what Emerson and Chai Kim (2018) call the seven model types for the creation of multiracial congregations. The first model is *neighborhood embracing*, in which the church purposefully reaches out to everyone in the neighborhood through mission and evangelism efforts. The second model type, *neighborhood charter*, speaks to the origin of the multiracial congregation: these congregations began as multiracial opposed to moving in this direction later. *Niche embracing* multiracial congregations are mission oriented, which leads to programming and outreach that draws people from across the region. *Niche charter* model types also originate as multiracial congregations and are mission driven. The fifth model type is *survival embracing*—multiracial congregations that intentionally shift from uniracial to multiracial in order to remain financially viable. *Survival merge* model types include congregations that become multiracial via the merging of two or more congregations. Finally, *mandated* multiracial congregations originate from decisions made by a denominational hierarchy external to the congregation.

MULTIRACIAL CHURCHES AND INEQUALITY

The ways in which inequalities and injustices are addressed and perpetuated within multiracial congregations also pose concern for multiracial congregations. Scholars find that the potential of a multiethnic congregation to address inequalities was diminished due to the way leaders and members reconstructed an organizational structure that was oppressive, including the tendency of church leaders to side with the interests of Whites when tensions arose (Edwards 2008a, 2008b; Jenkins and Dillon 2012). Further, they generally find that the rituals of worship for many of these churches mainly suit the desires of Whites (Edwards 2008b). Members of these churches valued visual representations of diversity (attendance of diverse members) and devalued other forms of diversity practices, thereby maintaining White socioreligious norms (Jenkins and Dillon 2012). This could include the utilization of Black bodies to perform Christian music while simultaneously denying those same Black bodies the opportunity to perform music from gospel genres. As a result, members of many of these multiracial congregations do not recognize systemic racial inequality and are unlikely to support civic and political efforts seeking to combat it (Dovidio, Gaertner, and Saguy 2015).

Within many multiracial churches, the rich diversity does not always make its way to the top of the organization, as racial minority group members tend to find themselves locked out of leadership and other positions of influence. Research shows that members of racial minority groups are often isolated, their concerns go unaddressed, and they do not have access to leadership positions (Christerson et al. 2005; Christerson and Emerson 2003; Edwards 2008b; Emerson and Smith

2000). Christerson et al. (2005) also find that members of the numerical majority group have a higher percentage of close friends within the congregation than numerical minority members do. This finding provides context for the isolation members of the minority group face and why they have shorter membership durations (Christerson et al. 2005; Scheitle and Dougherty 2010). Consequently, minority group members bear the highest relational costs of being involved in multiracial church organizations (Christerson et al. 2005). The emotional toll of being considered an "out-group" and the costs of forming subgroup spaces for these groups to socialize and worship are considerable and have lasting impact. Often, these minority groups must fundraise to financially support their needs (Christerson et al. 2015). Minority group members, who are often racial and ethnic minorities in general, face inequalities in both church and larger society that impact their lived experiences and mental and physical health.

Although there is much research devoted to how members of multiracial congregations interact (Christerson et al. 2005), worship together (Edwards 2008a, 2008b), and the role of White supremacy in these spaces (Jenkins and Dillon 2012; Dovidio, Gaertner and Saguy 2015), there is little to no research focused on how members and leaders of multiracial congregations may or may not use racialized frames when talking about complicated racial issues within the space and whether this leads to the reproduction of racism. There is also no research exploring how a multiracial church acts as a racialized organization that reproduces racial ideology through racialized practices and processes. This book attends to these omissions and limitations in the literature.

MULTIRACIAL CONGREGATIONS AND COLOR-BLIND RACISM STUDIES

According to Eduardo Bonilla-Silva (2018), color-blind racism emerged as the dominant racial ideology after the legislative and judicial gains of the civil rights movement in the 1960s. Contrasted with the Jim Crow racism that defined Black folks and other persons of color as biologically inferior, color-blind racism tends to be much more subtle in nature, often relying on abstract, seemingly nonracial reasoning to explain away persistent racial inequality and differential treatment. On the surface, color-blind rhetoric seems reasonable and even rational. It often appeals to those who believe it is in line with the teachings of the Reverend Dr. Martin Luther King Jr., who proclaimed in his 1963 March on Washington "I Have a Dream" address, "I have a dream that my four little children will one day live in a nation where they will not be judged by the color of their skin but by the content of their character" (King 1963). However, Bonilla-Silva (2018) argues that such an ideology may be as destructive as Jim Crow racism because it dismisses contemporary issues of racism and discrimination facing marginalized groups by using neoliberal arguments, thus maintaining the racial status quo without the racist vitriol of the past.

According to Bonilla-Silva (2018), the central component of any dominant racial ideology is its frames, or set paths for interpreting information. It is through these pathways or frames that individuals filter their experiences, emotions, and information to explain racial phenomena in predictable ways. He argues that there are four central frames that form the core of color-blind racism: abstract liberalism, naturalization, cultural racism, and minimization of racism. Specifically, the abstract liberalism frame uses ideas connected to political and economic liberalism to explain away racial inequality in seemingly nonracial ways. For example, segregated schools may be explained as a matter of individual choice, which ignores the history of de facto neighborhood segregation and discrimination in this country. For its part, the naturalization frame argues that racial differences are simply natural. Thus, issues like neighborhood segregation can be minimized without concern for being seen as racist. The cultural racism frame sees inequality as a result of cultural differences, for example, arguing that certain racial groups like to live in communities of people that look like them because it was how they were taught to live. Finally, the minimization of racism frame proposes racial inequality to be about individual decisions and not the result of contemporary group-based racism and discrimination.

Several studies have examined racial framing in multiracial congregational settings. For instance, Zerai (2011) conducted a multisite unobtrusive ethnography comparing three churches, in order to explore diverse meanings of church unity in the context of American color-blind society. Results from this study indicate that Site 1, a predominantly African American church, regularly challenged and worked to eradicate both color-blind racism and classism. This congregation placed special emphasis on liberation theology and regularly discussed the concept of social justice. Furthermore, Site 1's core values included the ideas of justice, liberation, and addressing the problem of the "color line." Finally, Site 1 had several justice-oriented ministries, which included direct social protest. Site 2, a multiracial congregation with a predominantly White leadership team, practiced a color-blind approach. Dominant racial ideology was evident in sermon content, leadership development, and structure. Over a period of six years, systemic racial inequality was not addressed in sermons. Although the church described itself as multiracial, race was rarely discussed, and despite the congregation being 30 percent Black, there were no African American pastors on staff. Site 3, an inclusive multiracial church with a diverse leadership team, worked to acknowledge and challenge color-blind racism as well as sexism, classism, and heterosexism. This urban, progressive church led by a female senior minister made multiple and consistent attempts to address micro-level and systemic racism through teachings, newsletters, and social justice activities (Zerai 2011).

The implications of this research led Zerai (2011, 269) to conclude that "unless multiracial congregations are actively involved in dismantling the racial hierarchy of the U.S., they are practicing color-blind racism." For Zerai, this dismantling involves multiracial churches developing what Bonilla-Silva (2003) defines as countercultures or oppositional views to the dominant racial ideology, colorblindness. While practicing colorblindness is only one racial project (Omi and Winant 2015) that acts to reproduce the racial status quo (see Mayorga-Gallo's [2019] work on diversity ideology or Carter and Lippard's work on racialized framing), it is a powerful one because it denies pernicious issues of racism and lays the blame for persistent inequality at the feet of Black folks and other people of color themselves (Carter and Lippard 2020).

Other scholars have also noted the deleterious impact of color-blind ideology in churches, both White and multiracial (Christerson et al. 2005; Emberson and Smith 2000; Marti 2005; Mehta et al. 2022; Oyakawa 2019). For instance, Michael Emerson and Christian Smith (2000) found that color-blind ideology is the dominant perspective among White evangelicals, with *abstract liberalism* serving as the dominant frame employed by these individuals. The deployment of abstract liberalism by White evangelicals is problematic because it allows for the freedom to deny the reality of discrimination based on racialized groups while also claiming to be not racist (Garces-Foley 2007a, 2007b). Similarly, Mehta et al. (2022, 639) found that White Christians "use colorblind religious frames and religious frames of diversity and inclusion to produce racial logics that overtly deny, minimize, or mystify the significance of racism."

In a similar study, which looked at Mosaic, a large multicultural evangelical congregation in Los Angeles, Gerardo Marti (2005) found its members engaged in a practice termed "ethnic transcendence." Through the strategic promotion of this practice, Mosaic effaces members' distinct ethnic identities and integrates members into its congregational culture, which rests squarely on the White popular culture of middle-class America (Garces-Foley 2007a, 2007b). Finally, Oyakawa (2019) interviewed multiracial pastors from the Religious Leadership and Diversity Project (RLDP) and found that racial reconciliation acts as a color-blind suppressive frame that limits the discussion of persistent racism and racial injustices. Findings from this study demonstrate that, even in multiracial contexts, pastors will attempt to placate White members at the expense of ignoring issues facing Black members.

With that being said, these studies reveal that multiracial churches are not immune to the impacts of racial ideology. Color-blind racism appears to permeate these spaces, resulting in the creation of White institutional space and deleterious effects that hurt Black church members in the end. Moreover, these studies also highlight what Bonilla-Silva (2018) stated so succinctly: "Racism can flourish even with no racist in sight," even in seemingly progressive multiracial spaces.

White Institutional Space

Wendy Leo Moore (2008, 165) defines White institutional space as the "integrated functioning of the racialized structures, cultures, and practices, as well as dominant ideologies and discourses of social institutions, which interact to create a totally whitewashed space." Specifically, Moore examines how law schools reproduce racism through White space. Laws schools, according to Moore, are the ultimate example of White space because of the interconnectedness of race and law, today and historically. This is typified through the sociolegal constructions of race, which Moore argues are connected to the conservation of White power, economically and politically.

Moore's findings show that these law schools are White spaces because of the characteristics of most occupants, normative structures, power hierarchy, and racial pathologies. In part, these White law school spaces reinforce Whiteness even through the art on the hallway and classroom walls. She notes that only one portrait of an African American judge, Thurgood Marshall, was exhibited on the walls of the schools she examined. The rest were White. Moore attributes this lack of White reflexivity to what Joe Feagin describes as the White racial frame, which can be defined as "an organized set of racialized ideas, images, emotions, and inclinations, which are closely connected to recurring discrimination and constitutive of still-racist institutions" (foreword by Joe Feagin in Moore 2008, xii). It is out of this frame that White institutional space is created and maintained.

The institutional nature of White space is intrinsically connected to the idea of institutional racism, which "captures how racist relations can be produced and reproduced without individuals' intentional racist acts, because racism is deeply entrenched within our institutions" (Moore 2008, 25). The effect of institutional racism is not relegated to law schools but can be found in every institution, including education, criminal justice, healthcare, and the media. There is no need to champion the work of Whites if their images and ideas are the only ones on display or being discussed. The simple inclusion of Whites and the exclusion of marginalized groups produces and reproduces White supremacy without any vitriol or overtly racist language. Institutional racism serves as the link between racial ideology and practices at the individual and institutional level. The result of this link is the reproduction of a racist social structure.

Bonilla-Silva (2018, 8) defines racial structure as the "totality of the social relations and practices that reinforce White privilege." As noted earlier, race as a social construct has very real and material implications. For example, "when race emerged in human history, it formed a social structure (a racialized social system) that awarded systemic privileges to Europeans (people socialized as 'White') over non-Europeans (people socialized as 'nonwhite')" (Bonilla-Silva 2018, 8). This kind of structuring gave birth to White supremacy, which accepts and rationalizes persistent racial inequalities. The racial structure, according to Williams (2020), not only materially advantages Whites but also allows for White cultural norms and practices to go unnamed and unquestioned.

There are two practical implications of the racial structure. First, it is maintained and defended because it provides privileges, rewards, and benefits for members of the dominant race. In the United States, Whites tend to reap the benefit of this system and enjoy the economic, political, and social benefits (Williams 2020; Thomas 2020; Weffer, Embrick, and Dominguez 2020; Durr 2020). Secondly, members of the subordinate group constantly struggle to change the racial narrative and structure because of the disadvantages and inequalities they face (Williams 2020; McDonald 2020; Durr 2020). Most certainly, Blacks and other people of color at the bottom of this racial structure suffer from the implications of structural racism (Embrick, Carter, and Lippard 2020; Lippard, Carter, and Embrick 2020). They fight not only against racial stereotypes and narratives that implicate them but also against destructive policies and practices that do not benefit them.

The reproduction of racist social structures is precisely the outcome of White institutional space. Moore's (2008) examination of White institutional space at elite law schools reveals at its core a foundation built on the exclusion of Black folks and other people of color. The result includes White accumulation of economic and political power and the construction of White norms, values, and ideological frameworks (Moore 2008), which impact every facet of the space, including sociocultural behaviors, acceptable notions of appearance and presentation, and classroom discussions. At the same time, although these law schools historically denied entrance to people of color, those barriers have in part subsided and people of color currently exist in these spaces, albeit underrepresented.

How does White institutional space proliferate when people of color are present? In the view of Moore (2008, 25), "Even in schools that are demographically nonwhite spaces, tacit White norms remain embedded in the school institution as a result of broader institutionalized racism in education." The institutional nature of White space is so inherent that it exists regardless of who occupies the physical space. Furthermore, the racists social structures that exists in these institutions are also permitted to reproduce based on the power holders, who are often White.

Moore (2008) notes that although her study is confined to elite law schools, the notion of White space can be applied to most U.S. institutions. This includes public spaces, neighborhoods, businesses, and communal areas. For example, Embrick, Weffer, and Dominguez (2019) explored the concept of White institutional space in museums. They found that White spaces are created, recreated, and maintained in elite museums through spatiality, the policing of space, and the management of access. And while White space pervades these institutions and spaces, there is an insidious and blatant aspect of White space that often legitimates White authority in very violent, atrocious, and sometimes deadly ways. Examples include the 2012 shooting death of Trayvon Martin in his own neighborhood by a neighborhood watchman and the social media rise of "Karens," in which White women attempt to police Black bodies by trying to keep them out of certain spaces. These instances of authority wielded by Whites were legitimized by White institutional space and move White racial ideology from theory to praxis, placing it within the same frame as the violent history of White supremacy in the United States (Onwuachi-Willig 2017; Elliott 2020).

That said, this book seeks to understand how White institutional space proliferates in a heterogeneous, multiracial space like WWC. As already articulated, White space does not depend on actors to be White or a space to be dominated by Whites for White supremacy to be reproduced; however, exploring the ways in which organizations that are supposed to embrace racial and cultural diversity within a religious context reproduce White space has important implications for both religion and society at large. The effect of White institutional space can be seen in White racial ideology, the "glue" that holds the racial structures together.

White Racial Ideology

Before exploring White racial ideology, it is important to understand racial ideology in general and its implications for the racial structure. Bonilla-Silva (2018, 9) defines racial ideology as "the racially based frameworks used by actors to explain and justify (dominant race) or challenge (subordinate race or races) the racial status quo." As he points out, the framework developed by Whites (the dominant group) becomes the main or master framework for ideological contestation. As Marx asserts in *The German Ideology*, "The ideas of the ruling class are in every epoch the ruling ideas, i.e. the class which is the ruling material force of society, is at the same time its ruling intellectual force" (Marx and Engels 1845 [2011], 169). Although subordinate groups develop their own frameworks, the framework of the dominant group serves as the foundation for the development of counterframes. As will be shown in later chapters, it is the development of these counterframes that contests racialization processes. According to Bonilla-Silva, racial ideology is characterized by looseness and flexibility and includes various elements such as common frames, style, symbols, stereotypes, and racial stories. This malleability allows the ideology to deflect and maneuver around facts and logic as well as accommodate the many structural locations of the actors who employ it.

A contemporary trend in race scholarship is the emergence of Whiteness studies. This field of research, which emerged in the 1990s, offered the idea of Whiteness as a "hidden identity." It is "hidden" because Whiteness does not intrude upon the everyday experiences of most Whites (Doane 2003). Unlike the case of Blacks and other people of color who are forced to contend with the consequences of their race daily, the hidden nature of Whiteness is a testament to White privilege. DuBois (1935) spoke of this privilege as the "public and psychological wage" enjoyed by even the poorest of Whites. Others have defined White privilege as "the unearthed benefits that flow to Whites in the American racial order—as well as the 'lack of awareness' of this privilege by Whites" (Doane 2003, 7). This privilege is the result of Whites' position at the top of the racial structure. White privilege can also be seen in the ways in which Whiteness is normalized across mainstream institutions. Whites are less likely to feel socially marginalized and experience prejudice and discrimination (Doane 2003; Gallagher 2020; Williams 2020), whereas Black folks and other persons of color often feel marginalized and discriminated against in various social contexts, including schools, health care, and the criminal justice system.

Williams (2020, 43) coined the term "White license," which he defines as a signification of "how people who imagine themselves to be White wield power through social, political, and economic institutions to control and direct their own and racialized Others' behavior and attitudes." According to this view, being White is not an inherent fact; rather, it is a product of social practices and White ideology. This "license" is obtained and secured through processes riddled by domination, willful acts, decisions, and policies directed at the racially oppressed (Leonardo 2004; Williams 2020). White license takes White privilege to another level in that privilege focuses on being while license explores the idea that Whites are granted the authority to *enact* bigoted and racist ways of thinking without punishment (Williams 2020). This results in a tangible system of oppression—White supremacy (Harris 1993; Williams 2020).

The racially unconscious dimension of Whiteness also poses consequences for White identity. There has been a decline in White ethnic designations among Whites (Gans 1979; Alba 1990; Doane 1997). This means that Whiteness is defined more through exclusionary practices and the labeling of otherness; in other words, Whiteness has come to be defined more by who is not considered White rather than by who is considered White. On the other hand, racial awareness can increase based on what Gallagher (1997) describes as "momentary minority" status, which is exposure to racialized environments and challenges to White dominance (Helms 1990; Tatum 1993). How White identity is defined, especially in juxtaposition to other racial groups, can be seen in multiracial spaces. How these racial groups and the issues they face are framed, handled, talked about or even minimized may be at the center of the reproduction of racism process.

Historically, "Whiteness" slowly emerged as a socially constructed identity in concert with the racialization of dispossession and enslavement resulting from ruling-class strategies to separate indentured servants and landless free persons based on race (Fields 1990; Allen 1994). Ruth Frankenberg (1993, 1) describes Whiteness as a "location of structural advantage," from which the racial "other" gets constructed. David Roediger (1994, 13) argues that Whiteness is nothing more than "the empty and therefore terrifying attempt to build an identity based upon what one is not and whom one can hold back." To be White is to be dominant, free, privileged, and positioned to subordinate "others."

Whiteness can subordinate the desires and practices of minority groups in multiracial churches (Edwards 2008b; Ince 2022). Furthermore, Whiteness can also frame conversations about race and ensure that those conversations do not take place. The effects of Whiteness in multiracial spaces does not stop with beliefs and views; they can also impact policies and practices, formal or informal (Moore 2008), which ultimately negatively impact the lived experiences of Black folks and other persons of color in these contexts. For an exploration of how Whites view themselves and their take on racism, let us turn to more contemporary studies on White racial identity.

White Racial Identity

Race is considered by many social scientists to be socially constructed and not based on any real biological differences (Cornell and Hartmann 1988; Omi and Winant 2015). The racial categorizing that results from these social constructions, however, hinges on things like ancestry and skin color, much of which is associated with biological factors. It must also be noted that this categorizing can change over time (Omi and Winant 2015). Consequently, Janet Helms (1990, 3) defines racial identity more abstractly as "a sense of group or collective identity based on one's perception that he or she shares a common racial heritage with a particular racial group." Blumer (1958) also frames identity within a group context, which he defines as the group position model. He argues that there are four elements in establishing group position: (1) a belief in in-group superiority (ethnocentrism); (2) out-group stereotyping; (3) proprietary claim over certain rights, resources, statuses and privileges; and (4) the desire of out-group members to have a greater share of those rights, resources, statuses, and privileges that are "understood" to "belong" to the in-group. This elucidates the idea that perception, self-identification, and group ties are key components of racial identity.

Some scholars pose that exploring Whiteness as an identity is essential to understanding the ways in which racial ideology is shaped and racism is reproduced. Whiteness, particularly in the United States, is associated with dominance. This dominance derives from Whites' position at the top of the racial structure. According to Bonilla-Silva (2018), "When race emerged in history, it formed a social structure (a racialized social system) that awarded systemic privileges to Europeans (the peoples who became 'White') over non-Europeans (the peoples who became 'nonwhite')" (8). For Bonilla-Silva (2018), this racial structure forms the core of White supremacy; as such, the maintenance of this structure reinforces privilege for Whites and inequalities for nonwhites. The sections that follow will examine scholarship around Whiteness, as we endeavor to understand the ways in which Whiteness has implications for multiracial spaces in terms of the inequalities that are reproduced even when Whites may not be in the majority.

MODELS OF WHITE RACIAL IDENTITY

Over the years, much research has been dedicated to understanding White racial identity (Helms 1990; Hardiman 1994; McDermott and Samson 2005; Rowe, Bennett, and Atkison 1994; Blumer 1958; Stoddart 2002). Helms (1993), for example, assumes that Whites are born the recipients and benefactors of racism, whether they realize it or not. For Whites to develop a healthy identity, Helms (1990) offers a theoretical six-stage model of White racial identity development. This includes (1) contact—ignorance in regards to the implications of race in the U.S.; (2) disintegration—racial consciousness; (3) reintegration—idealization of Whites and denigration of Blacks; (4) pseudo-independence—acknowledgement of one's own culpability in the perpetuation of racism; (5) immersion/emersion—attempt to become nonracist; and (6) autonomy—internalization of nonracist Whiteness and multicultural identity. This model leads one from the unknowing perpetuation of institutional racism to antiracism.

Hardiman (1994) advanced a similar theory, which moves from naiveté to nonracism:

Stage (1) naiveté—lack of racial awareness

Stage (2) acceptance—internalization and promotion of meritocracy, White supremacy, and the inferiority of "otherness"

Stage (3) resistance—unlearning of racism

Stage (4) redefinition—examination of privilege

Stage (5) internalization—anti-racism.

Both Helms' and Hardiman's theories have lately come under scrutiny. More contemporary studies of Whiteness and White identity have focused on intersectionality and have been interdisciplinary in nature (Hardiman and Keehn 2012). Since these theories were initially put forth, the number of people of color in the United States has dramatically increased and the election of the first Black president has shifted the ways in which we think about and "do" race. Between 2000 and 2010 alone, the country's Asian population grew by 46 percent and the Latinx population grew by 43 percent. Furthermore, the number of people who identify as multiracial is expected to increase from 7.5 million to 26.7 million between 2012 and 2060 (Progress 2050 2015). The rise of these populations challenges traditional notions of race as well as the Black-White binary.

As it relates to the models of White identity development, social scientists have critiqued their focus. According to Hardiman and Keehn (2012), "The models focus primarily on the racist attitudes and consciousness of Whites, and their views of people of color. Less attention, however, is paid to how Whites experience or name their own identity in a racialized society." White racial identity becomes even more complex when honorary Whiteness and the emerging racial order are considered and explored.

HONORARY WHITENESS AND THE NEW RACIAL ORDER

Although Whites still occupy the dominant position in the racial structure, according to social scientists, America's racial stratification system is changing rapidly (Bonilla-Silva 2018). According to Bonilla-Silva (2018), America's biracial order is atypical of the world racial system. He argues that, like many Caribbean nations and Latin American countries, the United States is moving from a biracial order to a triracial stratification system, albeit loose and complex. This triracial order is comprised of Whites at the top, "honorary" Whites occupying the intermediary position, and "collective" Blacks at the bottom. Bonilla-Silva (2018) suggests that the White group in the dominant position will include "traditional" Whites, new "White" immigrants, totally assimilated White Latinxs, lighter-skinned multiracial individuals and other subgroups. Honorary Whites, he argues, will comprise light-skinned Latinxs (i.e., most Cubans and some Mexican and Puerto Ricans), Japanese Americans, Korean Americans, Asian Indians, Chinese Americans, and most Middle Eastern Americans. Finally, at the bottom of this proposed triracial order, Blacks will include dark-skinned Latinxs, Vietnamese, Cambodians, Filipinos, most multiracial individuals, and Laotians.

The implications of this proposed triracial order are vast. First, it is apparent that skin color will become even more important in terms of distinguishing one's location in the racial order. Second, Bonilla-Silva (2018) argues that America will attempt to become in effect "post-racial," as Americans denounce calls to confront our country's racial past and make nationalist rhetoric more appealing. Furthermore, the new order will be more pluralistic and racially fluid. On the surface, this new racial order sounds more progressive than the existing one; however, according to Bonilla-Silva, it will continue to uphold White supremacy. This will be accomplished using the aforementioned nationalist appeals saturated in postracial, colorblind, and antiracial rhetoric. In the words of Bonilla-Silva (2018, 185), "Hence, in this emerging Latin America-like America, racial inequality will remain—and may even increase—yet there will be a restricted space to fight it." This restricted space will only reinforce Whites' position at the top of the racial order and ensure fewer race-based challenges to the existing status quo.

Indeed, there is evidence that the current racial order is moving in this direction. Statistics reveal that there are growing income, educational, occupational, and employment gaps between honorary Whites—light-skinned Latinxs and elite Asians—and collective Blacks (Bonilla-Silva 2018). This increasing inequality may serve as the foundation for honorary Whiteness to coalesce and lead to the early stages of group formation. According to Bonilla-Silva (2018), the members of this group may already be classifying themselves as White, developing White-like racial attitudes, and distancing themselves from members of the collective Black group. These trends are typified in Bonilla-Silva's (2018) findings, which show that 60 percent or more of the members of Latinx groups he regards as honorary Whites self-classify as White, while 50 percent or fewer of the members of the groups he regards as belonging to the collective Black category self-identify as Black. These trends are detailed in later chapters, as members of the WWC community reflect on their own identities.

Feagin (2013, 193) describes this group, noting, "There are some middle and upper-class Latinos who have adapted aggressively to White norms and folkways and accepted rather uncritically important aspects of the omnipresent White racial frame." This adaptation and honorary White status have compounded to create what Feagin (2013) has called a White-Hispanic or Hispanic "ethnicity" for the purpose of more fully assimilating into White institutions. While this seems to be an effort to evade the negative effects of being non-White in U.S. society, the new "ethnicity" also has a clear anti-Black affect.

It is important to note that Whites may begin making distinctions between honorary Whites and collective Blacks by becoming more favorable to the former group. Still, although Whites may develop more favorable attitudes toward honorary Whites, the dominant group still maintains the authority to mark both in-group and out-group boundaries, which will solely be based on Whites' wishes and practices (Bonilla-Silva 2018). Consequently, these "honorary" Whites are still subordinate to Whites, will face discrimination, and will not receive equitable treatment. At the same time, the benefits of honorary Whiteness outweigh their subordinate status. The first benefit lies in the close proximity to Whiteness, which affords more societal privileges. The second benefit is a distance from collective Blackness and the inequalities that accompany that social location.

Exploring honorary Whiteness is essential to understanding the ways in which White supremacy and racism are reproduced in multiracial spaces, including WWC. Considering the potential minority-majority status Whites may have in this space, honorary White ideology expands the scope of Whiteness. Individuals who may or may not be perceived or identify as White may indeed subscribe and reproduce White supremacy. The ways in which White identity and ideology converge has implications for space and the transformation of space into White institutional space even in a church that is multiracial.

Black/Latinx Identity and the Church

We have gone into detail exploring the confluence of Whiteness, White institutional space, the American religious landscape, and racism. Furthermore, we have also reviewed existing literature on multiracial churches, which argues that inequalities do exist in these spaces, including the subordination of ethnic identities and the elevation of White preferences over minority desires. For the purposes of this book's arguments, we believe it is also imperative to briefly summarize scholarship that examines Black and Latinx racial identity. The ways in which members of these groups identify impacts how they understand racial issues. These processes are more complex than it may appear on the surface.

As previously mentioned, social scientists pose that race is a social construct, the product of experiences and meaning-making (Cornell and Hartmann 1988; Omi and Winant 2015). Ethnicity, on the other hand, refers to cultural signifiers like nationality, language, religion, and food. According to the U.S. Census Bureau, a 1997 decision by the U.S. Office of Management and Budget requires five minimum racial categories—White, Black or African American, American Indian or Alaska Native, Asian, and Native Hawaiian or Other Pacific Islander, while recognizing two ethnicities: Hispanic and Latino (Humes, Jones, and Ramirez 2011). On the surface, the recognition of only two ethnicities might downplay the category's significance; however, Howard (2000) describes ethnic identity as fluid, evolving, and related to high self-esteem.

Although the American racial landscape has focused on the White-Black binary, this study seeks to understand topics associated with race in a south Florida multiracial congregation; therefore, the exploration of race and ethnicity must include Hispanics and Latinxs. Not considered a racial category, this designation reveals a complicated intersection of race and ethnicity. This is so much the case that Hispanics made up 97 percent of all those classified as "Some Other Race" in the 2010 census (Humes, Jones, and Ramirez 2011). This suggests that many Latinxs understand their identity to be complex and multidimensional, and that the current census racial categories are insufficient (Rodriguez 2000). Examining these racial and ethnic categories provides a baseline for comparing ways in which each group approaches racial ideology.

BLACK RACIAL IDENTITY

The foremost example of work on Black racial identity comes from Cross (1971), who argues for a five-stage model of identity development. This continuum moves from negative to positive self-identification. Many Americans place all Blacks in the same category—African American. With this homogenous thinking comes a monolithic understanding of the Black experience in America; however, there is research demonstrating that Blacks not only have different ethnic identities but also have different thoughts and experiences when it comes to race (Sellers et al. 1998; Demo and Hughes 1991; Smith and Moore 2000; Blau 2003; Lacy 2007; Hunt and Ray 2012; Waters 1990; 1999).

The conflation of race and ethnicity ignores the identities of those who consider themselves Black but not African American. These may include people from African of West Indian countries. Black immigrants make up approximately 9 percent of America's Black population (Anderson 2015). This number is only expected to grow, making ethnic Blacks a significant portion of the general population.

Blacks immigrating from other countries tend to bring with them different conceptions of race. For example, in the Caribbean, race is often thought of as a spectrum that spans between Black and White, with choices in between (Itzigsohn, Giorguli, and Vazquez 2005; Newby and Dowling 2007), in a way that is opposed to the American-based Black-White binary. Upon arrival, Black immigrants must reexamine their identities in the context of the U.S. racial system. Often, they feel as if they must assimilate into African American culture because of how they are physically perceived (Waters 1994 and 1999; Rogers 2001; Newby and Dowling 2007). Conversely, many Black immigrants understand the American racial hierarchy and African Americans position in it and therefore make a concerted effort to differentiate themselves from African Americans in an attempt to drive off negative stereotypes (Waters 1999; Bailey 2001). This is easier for recent immigrants who have distinctive features such as accents, and more cumbersome for children of immigrants, born in the United States. The implications of these ethnic nuances for this research are important. Of the Black-identifying members of the sample, approximately half are immigrants whose racial ideologies are vastly different from those of the African American members considered. Potentially, the complexity and nuance of Black racial identity can impact whether members of this racial group use color-blind frames and other elements of racial ideology.

LATINX RACIAL IDENTITY

Latinxs make up the largest minority group in the United States and according to estimates are poised to comprise 25 percent of the U.S. population by 2050 (Choi, Sakamoto, and Powers 2008). In the United States the term "Latinx" refers explicitly to ethnicity, applied to anyone of Spanish culture or origin (U.S. Census Bureau 2013). Since this term has been designated as ethnic, Latinxs can identify as any race. With that said, based on the 2010 census, 53 percent of all Latinxs self-identified as White and 37 percent identified as Other (Humes, Jones, and Ramirez 2011). While this may seem easy to understand on the surface, research suggests that the self-identification of Latinxs is a rather complicated process. Latinxs often have a hard time self-identifying due in part to the ways in which the U.S. government makes a distinction between race and ethnicity (Stokes-Brown 2012). This difficulty is reinforced by Latinxs' refusal to answer race and ethnic-based questions, selecting "Other" as a race or picking a traditional racial category instead (Wimmer 2007; Stokes-Brown 2012). Often, self-identification decisions are impacted by skin color, country of origin, culture, and generation in the United States (Kibria 2000; Rodriguez 2000; Vaquera and Kao 2006; Newby and Dowling 2007).

The differences within Latinx populations have been well documented (e.g., differences between Mexicans and Puerto Ricans); however, societal perceptions often seek to homogenize these individuals. This homogenization is due in part to how race and ethnicity are defined according to the stereotypes of physical appearance held by Whites (Kibria 2000). This benefits those Latinxs with phenotypic characteristics closer to those of Whites; therefore, Latinxs often attempt to self-identify in a way that may or may not conflict with how they are perceived by others. For example, many Cubans self-identify as White because their racial identities are closer to those of non-Hispanic Whites. Not only do phenotypic characteristics impact self-identification, Latinx immigrants' identity is also connected to their country of origin and their physical location in the United States (Newby and Dowling 2007). For example, if a Latinx immigrant looks White and settles in an area with many Whites, they are more likely to assimilate racially as White. Generation also impacts racial identity. Immigrants and second-generation Latinx Americans are more likely to self-identify as other, Asian, or no race, while third-generation Latinx Americans are more likely to select Black, White or Native American (Vaquera and Kao 2006). Over time, the generational offspring of immigrants are more likely to assimilate and choose normative and historical racial identities. Exploring this identity helps us understand the diversity in experiences, ethnicities, and racial ideologies of Latinxs. These findings will be described in detail in later chapters.

When we explore White, Black, and Latinx racialized identities it is clear they impact each group's racialized views. In understanding these views, it is also important to explore ethnic identities, which add further nuance to how individuals see themselves and the ideologies that shape their perceptions. Furthermore, wwc's location in south Florida and the ethnic and racial diversity that exists in this space cannot be separated from wwcs potential usage of racialized frames and other elements of racial ideology. This is not a simple matter of a multiracial church within the context of the Black-White binary; as will be seen in the following chapters, matters related to identity highlighted in this section have real implications for the racial ideology and practices of wwc.

Conclusion

Although still greatly segregated, America's religious landscape is increasingly filled with multiracial spaces. On the surface, these multiracial churches may be seen as a celebration of diversity and a "reflection of heaven." Upon further investigation, they are often riddled by problematic policies, as they uplift the virtues of diversity but lack a true commitment to that diversity in leadership and other areas. Furthermore, Whiteness and White space may even characterize these settings without an overabundance of White bodies, revealing the insidious nature of ideology and institutional racism (Edward 2008a, 2008b). In other words, the "house" may look different but the foundation may still be the same. The legacy of America's racism espoused by White Christians may still be at work amid the diversification of these spaces, which, particularly wwc, are primarily composed of Black, White, and Latinx identities. The complex nature of these identities is described above in order to add context to the data described in the next three chapters.

This book seeks, from an organizational perspective, to understand how racism is reproduced in wwc, a multiracial church located in south Florida. Although previous research suggests that racial inequalities, lack of conversation around systemic racism, and a nonpursuit of justice characterize multiracial churches, what we do not know is how these multiracial spaces reproduce racism through ideological frames and organizational policies and practices. Also, we still do not have a good idea of how this "most-racial" period of American history, which includes the 2016 election of President Trump and the death of George Floyd Jr., has impacted these multiracial spaces and the ways in which they "do," talk about, and frame racial ideology. Lastly, what the literature has not revealed is the multifaceted nature of White supremacy and racism. The ways in which these ideological frameworks appear is not singular, often combining racist ideology (e.g., colorblindness) with White space's policies and practices.

CHAPTER 2

Color-Blind Ideology and the Reproduction of Racism

Reflections from the First Author

"You're playing the race card": an infamous line that rings in my head after a heated classroom discussion. A professor had just used an inappropriate word, leaving many feeling uneasy and uncomfortable. Responding to this tension, several Black students demanded among other things that the professor issue a formal apology; however, we were met with resistance from White students citing reverse racism and demeaning our experience.

I did not know it then, but I have come to realize that this was one of many examples of color-blind racial ideology in action. In my previous reflection, I admitted to feeling uncertain as to whether I was a victim of racialized ideology or being celebrated. This confusion was the result of me being aware of old-fashioned racism but unaware of how colorblindness is symptomatic of an equally vicious and more profuse form of racial domination. Using cultural stereotypes and claims of reverse racism has a way of achieving the same results as the blatant type without the dirtiness of using certain language. It is my hope that this example, along with the data discussed in this chapter, will demonstrate how colorblindness sustains a racialized social system.

Introduction

Unlike the White church, the multiracial church is supposed to provide, in theory at least, a place of refuge for marginalized groups and a place for Whites to learn about the issues facing other groups. Is this the case with WWC? In this chapter, we explore if and how WWC members and leaders further racial unity and justice or if they instead reproduce existing racial ideology. Specifically, we focus on the narratives (e.g., frames) and styles they use to maintain or counter Whiteness and White supremacy in a multiracial church space. As noted earlier, recent research has raised concerns that such multiracial churches may actually reproduce the racial problems they are thought to fix (Edwards 2008a, 2008b, 2014; Okuwobi 2019; Oyakawa 2019).

In the social science literature, color-blind racism has received a great deal of attention. Scholars have gone to extensive lengths to show how it is employed to explain away the realities of racial inequalities and persistent forms of racism and discrimination (Carter and Lippard 2020; Burke 2016), thereby absolving Whites from any responsibility and upholding practices and policies that reproduce inequality. From humor (Perez 2017; 2022) to political speeches (Bonilla-Silva and Dietrich 2011) to classroom discussions on race and inequality (Stoll 2014) to Supreme Court debates on affirmative action (Carter and Lippard 2020; Carter, Lippard, and Barid 2019) and undocumented immigrants (Carter and Lippard 2015; Douglas, Saenz, and Murga 2015), to commentary on Hurricane Katrina (Shelton and Coleman, 2009) to conversations defining what racism is exactly (Doane 2006), color-blind rhetoric appears ubiquitous in the United States whenever issues of race are discussed.

Eduardo Bonilla-Silva (2018), the James B. Duke Distinguished Professor of Sociology at Duke University and leading scholar in the area, argues that color-blind racism gives Whites the ability to rationalize minorities' contemporary status and plight as products of market dynamics, naturally occurring phenomena, and Blacks' imputed cultural limitations (e.g., lack of work ethic), all while minimizing the role of institutional discriminatory policies and practices. Moreover, he argues that the shield of colorblindness gives Whites the freedom to "express resentment toward minorities; criticize their morality, values, and work ethic; and even claim to be victims of 'reverse racism'" (Bonilla-Silva 2018, 4) without being described as racist. Most interesting about this deleterious perspective is that propagators of color-blind racism can appear or truly believe themselves to be nonracist, mislabeled, or even victims themselves.

If this mislabeling is true and everyone claims to be antiracist, how does a racist system characterized by biased practices and policies and abject inequality remain firmly intact and viable in the United States today? Bonilla-Silva (1997, 2018) and numerous other scholars (Doane 2006; Embrick et al. 2020; Feagin 2013; Gallagher 2020; Moore 2008; Omi and Winant 2015) argue that the answer to the riddle is found in a racialized social system where racial oppression is baked into societal structures, policies, and practices. As constructed, no racist is needed to produce and reproduce the racial status quo if we ignore the broader structural conditions and believe them to be unbiased. In this light, it is no surprise that an emphasis on who is or who is not a "racist" is not as important as uncovering the structural and ideological nature of racism and may actually hinder the needed work to make meaningful change.

Before getting into the purpose and findings of this chapter, we would like to first note responses of interest that remind us of the ideological conundrum faced by church members, leaders, and really all ordinary citizens acculturated in such a system. During the interviews, among other questions, we asked three questions about racism as a concept and racism in practice. We asked the interviewees to define racism and give a contemporary example of the phenomenon. We also asked if organizations (schools, churches, employers, social clubs, etc.) could be defined as racist. Finally, we asked if the respondent felt race/racism can no longer be used as an "excuse" for lack of success in society. These questions were designed to understand racial ideology and to clarify whether this ideology included elements of colorblindness.

Of those interviewed, no one gave institutional, systemic, or structural definitions of racism; however, systemic racism was referenced by three interview participants (all of whom identify as White) at some point during their interviews. The overwhelmingly micro-level or individualistic understandings of racism by these interview participants speaks to the proliferation and dominance of an ideology that locates inequality at the individual level (e.g., lack of work ethic) and not at the institutional level (Carter and Corra 2012; Carter et al. 2014).

The fact that so few would reference institutional or systemic racism and relied on individual explanations instead speaks to a broader problematic ideology in the United States regarding race, including that described by Bonilla-Silva (2018). It suggests that many people still buy into aspects of old-fashioned racist ideology that blames marginalized groups, including Black folks, for their own suffering and hardships. The existence of such views should not be seen as arbitrary or trivial. There has been concerted pushback recently (e.g., new laws banning the teaching of critical race theory and diversity, equity, and inclusion [DEI] initiatives; political rhetoric; and legal rulings on programs such as affirmative action and voting rights protections) and historically to eliminate discussion or even acknowledgement of systemic racism and injustices (Lati 2021). Furthermore, the lack of engagement with systemic/institutional racism also means that many people who employ color-blind racist rhetoric may be passively doing so without understanding the implications of this ideology. Finally, it is important to note that the dominant racial ideology does *not* rely on certain groups, whether they be Republican or Democrat or Black or White because it transcends race or any other category, often being reproduced by those who are most negatively impacted.

While Bonilla-Silva notes that most Whites employ color-blind ideology, it is not exclusive to Whites. Others employ elements of colorblindness as a part of their racial ideology as well, particularly people of color who use their "honorary" Whiteness as a tool to benefit from the racial structure or people who simply subscribe knowingly or unknowingly to White supremacy (Bonilla-Silva 2018). For example, Cox (2021) found that millennials of color (MOC) indeed utilized the frames of color-blind racism, although in more nuanced, inconsistent, and contradictory ways and less than their White counterparts. The notion that non-Whites utilize these very micro-level understandings of race and racism speaks to the frames that form the core of colorblindness and the dominance of racial ideology in the United States today.

One of the goals of this book is to understand if and how members and leaders of WWC used color-blind frames and styles in ways that reproduce racism. These frames have been shown to be foundational in the thinking of most Whites and some non-Whites regarding issues of race and racial inequality. However, in the chapter that follows, we will move past these frames and describe other framing techniques used by members and leaders of the church to minimize the need to discuss and act on issues of race, racism, and racial injustices. Before doing that, we describe how our participants used color-blind frames as articulated by Bonilla-Silva (2018) when discussing issues of race and racism.

"No, I'm Not Racist"—Dealing with the Racist Label

It should be apparent by now that the current study of race and racism is shifting its emphasis from micro-racial aggressions to more structural understandings of racism by intentionally moving away from the "racist" label, which has historically focused on individual micro-aggressions and ignored the institutional nature of racism (Doane 2017; 2020; Embrick, Carter, and Lippard 2020; Embrick et al. 2020; Williams 2020; Gallagher 2020). Bonilla-Silva (2018) made it clear from chapter 1 of his seminal work that he is not interested in pointing at individuals and labeling them as racist; rather, he wrote, "Because this book is anchored in a structural understanding of race relations, my goal is to uncover the collective practices (in this book, the ideological ones) that help reinforce the contemporary racial order" (14).

To label certain people as racist or nonracist detracts from Bonilla-Silva's argument concerning the institutional and systemic nature of color-blind ideology. Instead, one must look at the racial order and how it is maintained, which allows actors to see the role they play in maintaining this order instead of dismissing racism as a thing of the past or using their relationships with people of color to promote their supposed antiracism. Similarly, the aim of this book is not to label any congregant or congregational leader as "racist," nor to refer to them as "good" or "bad," Christian or unchristian. Instead, we focus on whether (or not) leaders and members of a multiracial church are perpetuating (or contesting) this ideology. Like non–church members, these individuals were socialized in a society that teaches this racial ideology, which benefits one group over others. We now shift to demonstrating how staff and volunteers use color-blind frames in thinking about race, racism, and prominent racialized events.

The Frames of Color-Blind Racism

We have already noted that Bonilla-Silva (2018) has identified four central frames that form the core of color-blind racism: abstract liberalism, naturalization, cultural racism, and minimization of racism. These dominant racial frames provide the intellectual road map used by the dominant group to navigate the always rocky road of domination.[1]

ABSTRACT LIBERALISM

Abstract liberalism can be described as the central frame of color-blind racism. This frame "involves using ideas associated with political liberalism (e.g., 'equal opportunity,' the idea that force should not be used to achieve social policy) and economic liberalism (e.g., choice, individualism) in an abstract manner to explain racial matters" (Bonilla-Silva 2018, 56). Relying on this frame allows Whites to oppose approaches aimed at dealing with racial inequality while appearing moral, practical, or reasonable. For example, many Whites oppose affirmative action based on the argument of equal opportunity, which posits that no group should receive preferential treatment and that all individuals should have equal opportunity based on merit. This is an example of color-blind racism because it fundamentally ignores systemic and structural racism that has precluded minorities from accessing traditionally White spaces and pretends that equality has been achieved (Carter and Lippard 2020; Carter, Lippard, and Baird 2019). Research in the social sciences finds principles of abstract liberalism to be problematic in debates over other racial issues as well, including immigration policies, in which it is deployed to frame people of color as undesired and unqualified for U.S. citizenship (Carter and Lippard 2015; Douglas, Saenz, and Murga 2015).

As previously stated, one of the hallmarks of abstract liberalism is the idea that Whites are not responsible for the inequalities experienced by Black folks or other people of color. This ideology can be seen in several of the statements made by members of WWC. For example, Kal, a twenty-five-year-old White male, full-time staff member who serves as a campus worship leader, acknowledged systemic racism while denying any culpability for himself and his "lineage." He states, "I am always so sorrowful that we were a part of a huge problem. Even though it wasn't necessarily my lineage or things like that, it's still a systemic problem that a part of my color has made a huge issue, and made people lesser than how they should feel, lesser than what they are." Kal went on to say, "I know I wasn't a part of the problem. I didn't do certain things or whatever." Kal's acknowledgment of systemic racism contradicts how he understands his role (and the role of his ancestors) related to the consequences of systemic racism. The logical extension of this line of thinking is that others are the problem, not him, ignoring the ways in which he may be complicit in the reproduction of institutional racism.

Arthur, a White/Hispanic male in his mid-thirties who volunteers in guest services, also gave voice to the notion that Whites are not responsible for systemic inequalities. He stated, "Oh, you're in a place. Now, you're the minority, but we're blaming everything on the White man. It's like, 'whoa, whoa, whoa, whoa, whoa. Time out. Not all White people are the same, just like not all Black people are the same." He went on later in the interview to state, "Stop blaming the 'superior race,' start doing something about it so you're up there." Not only does Arthur disavow the idea that Whites are responsible for the many inequalities people of color face, we also see the components of new racism form here. In describing contemporary or new racism, contemporary race scholars have noted that explanations for the causes of inequality have shifted over time from biological explanations to cultural ones (Bobo and Kluegel 1997; Bobo and Tuan 2006; Carter and Corra 2012; Kinder and Sanders 1996; Schuman et al. 1997). More specifically, per Bonilla-Silva (2018, 7), new racism "encompasses an ideology that blames Blacks themselves for their poorer relative economic standing, seeing it as the function of perceived cultural inferiority."

In his interview responses, Arthur is advocating that minorities should take responsibility for their economic and social positioning. He further reinforces the notion of new racism when he gives the following example: "You have the people that grew up in poverty or didn't have jobs or parents didn't have a college education, things like that, they're all the way in the back. It's like, 'Okay, in the race of life, this is where you guys are starting.' So, I shouldn't be trying to trip the guys in the front. I should be trying to train the people in the back. I think that's one of the things that, as a culture, we miss out on. We're too busy pointing fingers." The people being described by Author are by and large minorities who disproportionately suffer from poverty and unequal access to quality education (Oliver and Shapiro 1995; Blank 2001; Council of Economic Advisors 1998). In his view, their starting position in life is a simple fact of life, not attributable to any forces, systems, or institutions. He also suggests that those in the back have a responsibility to not point at the systems that caused them to start there; rather, they should assist those who are even further behind.

Arthur's statements speaks to the ideology of individualism, a key component of abstract liberalism (Bonilla-Silva 2018). American individualism emphasizes each person as an "individual" with "choices." This principle is used to justify housing segregation, inequality in our education systems, and other negative racial outcomes. According to Bonilla-Silva (2018, 63), "Individualism today has been recast as a justification for opposing policies to ameliorate racial inequality because they are 'group based' rather than 'case by case.'" In his interview, Arthur emphasized the idea that one can do something about their individual material condition, deflecting attention away from systemic, structural and institutional policies and practices that produce inequalities. Bonilla-Silva (2018, 63) summed up the idea of individualism: "If minority groups face group-based discrimination and Whites have group-based advantages, demanding individual treatment for all can only benefit the advantaged group." Arthur's model of placing responsibility for one's status squarely on one's shoulders falls in this category of the abstract liberal frame.

In our findings, the use of the abstract liberalism frame was not just relegated to White participants but was found among Black leaders of the church as well. For example, Melissa Del Rio, a thirty-seven-year-old Black woman and full-time campus ministry leader, used it to differentiate herself from other Black women who attended her high school. She stated, "So I didn't have that desperation, rat race, crab in a barrel mentality, because I was like, 'I'm here. I made it on my own merit." Melissa here employs merit ideology, core to the abstract liberalism frame, as an explanation to justify her positionality in that space as well as a tool of differentiation from other Black women.

Mike, a forty-one-year-old campus pastor who racially identifies as "Other" and ethnically identifies as Puerto Rican, also used the abstract liberalism frame when describing racial progress. When discussing President Obama's historic election, Mike stated, "And I think that it does remove some level of excuse because if one person can do it, so can another, and another, and another." Mike went on to say, "President Obama and people being in high levels of leadership and authority in a position, I do think that it does begin to say, 'Look, those things can tend to be excuses because if this handful of people can do it, then so can others.'" While Mike acknowledged earlier in the interview that race and racism persist and are problematic, he simultaneously argued against the notion that they are the reasons why people are not successful in life. Sydney, a Black female in her fifties from Jamaica, used similar language to describe how she sees race, racism, and its impact on people of color. She posed, "I do agree that we cannot use the excuse of race as to why we don't succeed because we've seen President Obama succeed, Clarence Thomas succeed." Highlighting the successes of a biracial man and a politically conservative jurist, respectively, in no way suggests that all Black and brown people will be afforded the same opportunities. Pointing to the salience of race while ignoring the social outcomes of race and the inequalities people of color face because of race further solidifies the position of Whites atop the racial structure, protects their privilege, and further aids in the subordination of minorities.

NATURALIZATION

The naturalization frame allows Whites to explain away racial phenomena by suggesting they are natural occurrences and not the result of systemic or institutional structures that benefit White folks at the expense of marginalized groups. Bonilla-Silva (2018, 56) argues that thanks to this frame, Whites can claim "segregation" is natural because people from all backgrounds "gravitate toward likeness." These preferences, related to everything from housing to relationships, are framed as nonracist and a reflection of the "natural" order. Within multiracial churches, assumptions based on this frame may be used to describe racialized events as naturally occurring, as opposed to being the consequences of the racial structure and the reproduction of racism on the part of church leaders and the wider church community.

For example, when asked where he was from, Kal described his home church and community in the following way: "It was just predominantly White, where I grew up. It's not even necessarily, especially now, I don't think it was intentional. I think it's just honestly from centuries of how we grew up, you know? Or how that town and everything grew up, at least in the place where I was growing up." When reflecting on the lack of diversity in his hometown, he pointed to history without contextualizing it and acknowledging the institutional racism and residential segregation practices that gave rise to the local lack of diversity. Furthermore, when asked if organizations can be racists, Kal stated, "So, going to the question, I'm trying to say it doesn't necessarily mean, if a place is predominantly Black or predominantly White or predominantly Latino or predominantly these things, it doesn't mean that they're necessarily racist. It might just be a byproduct of where their community is and all these different things." Again, Kal used the naturalization frame to justify contemporary racial dynamics, implicitly justifying segregation as natural and not the result of racialized ideology.

Cata, a White female ministry leader volunteer in her mid-twenties, used the naturalization frame to describe social dynamics within WWC. Speaking of the merging of people and cultures from the church's downtown location with those of the southwest location, she stated, "There's downtown and then there's southwest. I don't think it's a mean thing and I don't think either side feels like, 'Oh, they don't want to be with me,' it's just where they naturally fall, I guess." She went on to say, "You can see that they can love each other and appreciate each other but they don't actually care to hang out . . ." Over the course of the interview, Cata described the two church campuses as having different cultures, which in her view naturally explained the segregation which happened when the two campuses came together at the southwest location.

Kal also used the naturalization frame to describe the impact of community demographics on a church's racial makeup. When asked whether organizations can be racist, Kal replied:

> I think that there are churches that make it exclusive and then they become racist, but I think also it depends on where the church is located, you know? The reason why I say it stems deeper is sometimes maybe the church is in an area that was a predominantly White population, and so what you're going to get is, mostly within the community that you are serving and that you are taking care of, that you're loving, it is going to be predominantly White people. I would think it would be weird to be like, "Okay, let's go bus 30 miles down the road, where there's another community already loving and serving these people, just to make ourselves feel better, let's bring in some Black people, or different races, to make us feel better." I feel like that would be even worse. I think it would almost stem the problem more. That's why I say it's a little bit deeper.

According to Emerson and Chai Kim (2018), there is a relationship between diverse churches and diverse communities; however, Kal argued that churches are naturally the byproduct of the community in which they are housed. Again, this ignores housing segregation and the institutionally racist practices that lead to neighborhood homogenization. Furthermore, Kal's use of the naturalization frame argues against some of Emerson and Chai Kim's (2018) model types related to the formation of multiracial congregations, particularly the survival embracing, survival merge, and mandated model types discussed in chapter 1. All of these model types intentionally seek to transform uniracial churches into multiracial churches. According to Kal, this type of mission would be self-serving and worse than homogeneity.

We found the naturalization frame also used in describing the racial makeup of the wwc campuses. Grace, a thirty-one-year-old White female ministry leader, employed it to describe northwest campus: "Our newer campus, northwest, is positioned in a very Hispanic community, so most people that go to that campus are mostly Hispanic. I guess it's just the neighborhood, the community." Hojuma, at eighty-five the oldest interview participant and a volunteer small group leader, similarly commented, "I live near the northwest campus, and it is probably more Hispanic because that's the area around that campus." For his part, Mac, a thirty-eight-year-old White staff leader who oversees one of the ministries for all the campuses, pointed to the problematic nature of the naturalization frame, particularly related to the northwest campus:

> It's a conversation where we're going to plant a church in a Hispanic community and we would never consider somebody who is Black because the Hispanic community wouldn't take well to them. I've had that conversation multiple times, and I specifically had it when we opened up our northwest location. The city is highly, highly Hispanic. It's just as . . . I can't remember, 40–50 percent of people are only speaking Spanish. So, the conversation didn't turn from he or she doesn't speak Spanish. It was the conversation about I don't know how well Hispanic people are going to take to Black folks. . . . The best player that we had on our team that could go and run that campus was a Black guy and we wouldn't consider him.

Thus, three people describing this wwc campus recognized that its large Hispanic population was a direct result of the surrounding community. The naturalization frame was not only used to justify this observation but also to justify why a Black clergy person wouldn't be a good fit to lead the congregation. In this example, the naturalization frame is a tool used to reproduce institutional racism, thereby limiting the professional opportunities of Blacks.

Mike, a campus pastor who identifies as Puerto Rican, also used the naturalization frame to describe the staff demographics of wwc. He noted, "We are in south Florida, and there's a heavy Latino population, Hispanics. So, there are a lot of Hispanics on staff," further giving credence to Mac's critique of staff hires, especially regarding the northwest location. Furthermore, Hans, the campus pastor for the southwest location, described how the naturalization frame reproduces racism when he said, "If you put only White people on stage, you're probably going to have a predominantly White congregation. If you put only Black people on stage, you're probably going to have a predominantly Black congregation." The decision to restrict a Black person from leading this campus is an extension of Hans' ideology. The congregation is a natural extension of the community, and the leadership of a congregation should be an extension of the people who attend. In this vein, it is only "natural" for the church to look like the community and "natural" for those in leadership to look like the people in the pews. The racist nature of this frame can be seen in the lack of attention to the dynamics that created this racialized community as well as to how leaders are restricted or elevated based on their race.

Jake, a fifty-nine-year-old White male who is married to a Black woman and volunteers as a small group leader, acknowledged the potential role of systemic racism in relation to the naturalization frame:

> So, if an organization, now it might not be their own fault, and it may be, but that organization is in a predominantly White area or on the other spectrum a predominantly Black area, and it's a predominantly Black organization or White, there could be systemic racism underlying that they don't even realize just because people groups like to be together with their people. That's why the church had the hardest time integrating because it's just more comfortable to, I guess, be with your same kind of people. So I think, yeah, there's racism in and organizations and underlying racism that maybe organizations don't even realize.

When asked if organizations could be racist, Jake utilized the naturalization frame as an example to essentially answer in the affirmative. Although Jake did not explicitly assert that organizations intentionally engage in systemic racism, he did acknowledge the preference to be with racially similar people groups can be racist in and of itself. Although on the surface naturalization seems to describe "natural" relations and affinity with members of the same racial group, the examples given here demonstrates that at WWC it can reproduce racism through hiring decisions and the subordination of the interests and needs of some groups.

CULTURAL RACISM

Bonilla-Silva (2018, 56) defined cultural racism as a "frame that relies on culturally based arguments such as 'Mexicans do not put much emphasis on education' or 'Blacks have too many babies' to explain the standing of minorities in society." In other words, minorities are themselves to blame for their social standing because of misplaced morals or incorrect values. As biological explanations of racial inferiority have faded, cultural explanations of inferiority have risen in their place. Unfortunately, many of these culturally based arguments are not factually correct; however, as Bonilla-Silva (2018) has argued, these notions are malleable, often conflicting, but still used to legitimate existing systems of racial domination.

Exploring the ways in which this frame is utilized presents a better understanding of how racism is reproduced, even within a multiracial church setting.

Scholars have argued that the interracial contact experienced in multiracial congregations meets a sufficient number of conditions prescribed in Gordon Allport's (1954) contact hypothesis. This contact fosters more progressive attitudes on a variety of social issues (Johnson and Jacobson 2005; Yancey 1999, 2001, 2006). Further, it has been argued that interracial contact within religious settings has been more consistently linked with a reduction in racial prejudice and social distance than in most other contexts (Emerson 2006; Irving 1973; Johnson and Jacobson 2005; Leacock, Deutsch, and Fishman 1959; Parker 1968; Yancey 1999, 2001, 2006). Based on this research, one may suppose that the utilization of the cultural frame in a multiracial church context would be significantly reduced because of the level of multiracial contact; however, our findings reveal that at least in the case of the WWC, the cultural racism frame is used significantly both within and outside of the congregational space.

Alyssa, a fifty-year-old Asian American woman who serves on the ALT utilized the cultural racism frame in describing her past professional experiences. She commented, "When I was in retail for ten years and I was a district manager . . . all associates I had, were primarily Latin . . . I would always hear from some Latin communities or Latin friends of mine. They're like, well, they're very discriminant. They're very discriminant with other cultures." Here, Alyssa's use of the cultural racism frame to describe Latinxs as "discriminant" seemed to be affirmed by members of that very community, increasing the likelihood that she applies this notion to all members of Latinx communities. Likewise, Cata also used stereotypes to characterize Cubans, claiming, "Cubans are very racist. Cubans are super racist." Despite contact with Latinxs professionally, personally, and at WWC, strong stereotypes about this community persisted in these individuals' minds.

Cata also used the cultural racism frame to describe experiences outside of WWC. For example, she shared, "My school was considered, I guess, middle class growing up. It was by the rich public schools. They would call us the 'ghetto team,' on the sports stuff, and then there's always a more ghetto team. Mine was a lot of Hispanics and Brazilians, I guess, that went to our school. Then, there was the other one that was more inner city that was right next door. So, it's all relative." Cata used the cultural racism frame to describe the "inner city" team as more "ghetto." The implications of these terms are vast, in that they are often used in reference to Blacks (Doggett 2015; Logan et al. 2015). Although Cata acknowledged that her team was demeaned because of the presence of minorities, she replicated this same kind of marginalization when referring to a team that was more than likely composed of majority Black athletes.

Hojuma also used the cultural racism frame to describe past professional experiences when asked to reflect on her identity as a White person. Hojuma, unlike most interviewees, immediately began discussing the idea of White privilege, a term in which she had just become familiar. She linked her privilege to an experience as an assistant principal at a predominantly White school that was being mandated by the federal government to merge with a predominantly Black school. Upon discovering that some of the Black students had undiagnosed learning difficulties, she stated:

> Now, that Black school was not in a ghetto area. It was in the area that the professional Blacks lived in. The teachers, we had to move teachers also, and the Black teachers, a lot of them live in that community. The dentists, the doctors, the professional Blacks. A lot of them lived in that community . . . And when I worked with some teachers who were Black, I had some excellent Black teachers, some of the best teachers I had. But I had some others who, you know, they couldn't even alphabetize. You would ask them to turn their records in alphabetical order or something, I had an assistant principle who didn't alphabetize. And I had to think "Okay, don't be judgmental here, because they didn't have the advantage that you had." This was not important in their school, evidently.

Hojuma utilized the cultural racism frame in a few nuanced ways. First, she distinguished that the Black school was not in the "ghetto", suggesting that had it been in the ghetto, this would have provided an appropriate context for the students' learning difficulties as well as the teachers' skill sets or lack thereof. Second, although she acknowledged that the teachers live among the Black middle class, she assumed based on skin color that they have been disadvantaged. Last, she also assumed that alphabetization was not important at the Black school, without understanding how they structured their documentation. These stereotypes about Blackness are emblematic of cultural racism.

Chris, a thirty-three-year-old campus pastor who identifies as Native Hawaiian and Pacific Islander, also expressed stereotypes about Blackness. In providing examples of injustices he has witnessed, he argued for what he sees as the biggest injustice in Black communities: "Because I have successful Black friends, but when I look at their situation where they come from, they come from a home environment where I think the biggest injustice to the Black community or to the minority community is a lack of male fathers, of a male presence . . . I think the biggest injustice to the impoverished community, or say the community I grew up in or the Black community, if you will, would be a lack of a father-figure before anything else." Although statistics demonstrate that Black children (57.6 percent) experience fatherlessness at higher rates than Hispanic (31.2 percent) and White children (20.7 percent), the numbers are still high in White communities (Vespa, Lewis, and Kreider 2013). Despite such high rates across racial groups and the finding that Black fathers tend to spend as much or more quality time (e.g., reading or playing) with their children as their White counterparts (Jones and Mosher 2013), a common stereotype of Black communities is the absence of fathers. This is often used in a derogatory manner and in ways that lack context. These stereotypes are often used without mention of the overrepresentation of Black males in the criminal justice system (Miller and Garran 2007; Hawkins 2001) and the lack of quality healthcare access that leads to poorer health outcomes for Black males (Joiner 2004).

There were also many examples of this frame being used to describe racialization processes within the context of wwc. Alyssa employed it to describe the process of translating English into Spanish during the worship experiences: "And I remember I was educated, you got to bring on the right translator because it's got to be a Colombian, because they're going to communicate right. They're educated, and like, 'Oh, if you say it the wrong way, you're going to lose the respect of the Venezuelans' . . . there's even this class discrimination of we're better than you within the Latin field." Although Alyssa went on to affirm that she has never witnessed this at wwc, she did acknowledge that she was told this by another staff person at the church. Whatever the case may be, she asserts here the idea that one subset of Latinxs are smarter than others and further perpetuates the notion that Latinxs consistently discriminate and harbor prejudice against one another.

Craig James, a twenty-eight-year-old Black male from Jamaica who serves on a campus praise and worship team, described the use of the cultural racism frame by others at wwc: "For young people who are Black, especially the young Black males, they have approached me a lot more willingly and sometimes started out by saying, 'It's good to see an upstanding, intelligent, talented Black man around' . . . I've had those kinds of statements said from teenagers all the way up to grown persons who are also in leadership." Bonilla-Silva (2018) acknowledged that color-blind racist frames can indeed be used by people of color, as seen here. The individuals Craig refers to seem surprised by his appearance and demeanor, as if they had never previously encountered a professional Black man. To them, Craig stood out in contrast to the many negative stereotypes that persist concerning Black males, who are seen as lazy, uneducated, and thugs. The surprise conveyed by the Black males signified an internalization of these stereotypes as well. The use of this frame by the staff, volunteers, and members of wwc could further be seen in another example directed toward Craig. He stated, "After engaging in conversation, a woman who I believe was White, she said, 'Wow. For a Black man, you speak so well.' And the truth is that she really believed that she was offering me a compliment, which goes to show you how deeply rooted sometimes racial slurs, and racial classifications, and racial perspectives of people are embedded in just the way how we speak to each other and view each other." This is a clear example of the cultural racism frame directed toward a Black man. Because of Craig's racial identity, the woman seemingly expected him to be inarticulate and incapable of utilizing grammatically correct speech. This is surprising, considering the countless public examples of professional Black men in the news media, government, and other public forums and speaks to the malleable nature of color-blind ideology, which shifts and contorts itself seemingly at will. This includes ignoring examples that discredit this frame and embracing every instance that seemingly supports it. Moule (2009) referred to the term "refencing" to describe the process of receiving evidence that confronts deeply held and usually unrecognized biases. When this confrontation happens, the human brain usually finds ways to return to familiar stereotypes.

Perhaps the most alarming use of this frame by an interviewee occurred in the joint interview with Cata and Arthur, a wife and husband who both identify as White. It is important to note that Cata serves as a volunteer ministry leader and Arthur serves as a volunteer in a ministry. In highlighting the diversity of the southwest location, Cata and Arthur described a group they consider to be "Nigerians."

> **Arthur:** Where are these guys from? I think they're Nigerian but they come with the-
> **Cata:** Yeah, like legitimately Nigerian.
> **Arthur:** . . . Nigerian dress and all that and they come.
> **Cata:** Full garb. Super cool.
> **Arthur:** I'm pretty sure either they're all family or they all know each other. They roll up and, like, a dozen of them come together every Sunday.
> **Cata:** And they're probably not even really American.
> Like, they're Nigerian, Nigerian. I don't even know if they have citizenship yet, to be honest with you. I don't know.

Cata's and Arthur's use of this frame was blatant and dripping with color-blind racism. First, the ethnic identity of the people they described was assumed to be Nigerian. Not once did Cata and Arthur confirm that they definitely knew the ethnic identity of the individuals they were describing. Perhaps they assumed it to be Nigerian because that may be the African country with which they are most familiar. Second, they also initially assumed that members of this group are related to each other. This may have been inaccurate. Finally, Cata and Arthur both reinforced the supposed ethnic identity of these individuals by referring to them as "legitimately" Nigerian and "Nigerian, Nigerian." They then connected this notion of a strong ethnic identity to this group being non-American. A corollary of these assumptions was the idea that if one were to have a strong ethnic identity, they couldn't also be American. This further perpetuated the notion that to be White is to be American and to be American is to be White (Devos and Banaji 2005). Perhaps if they did not wear traditional African garb, the citizenship of this group would not have been called into question. Here, Cata and Arthur clearly rely upon stereotypes to support the cultural racism frame.

MINIMIZATION OF RACISM

Bonilla-Silva (2018) described minimization of racism as a frame that suggests discrimination is no longer a central factor affecting minorities' life chances (e.g., it's better now than in the past, or there is discrimination, but there are plenty jobs out there). Because the physical ravages of slavery are in days past or the fire hoses and police dogs of the civil rights movement have faded away, Whites can now claim that racism is over. This frame can be found when Whites accuse minorities of "playing the race card" and speaks to the heart of what many Americans call a "post-racial" society. The growing number of multiracial churches is also evidence for those who subscribe to this ideology.

Like the other frames, this frame was also utilized by members of WWC. In describing the fallout from the NFL protests led by Colin Kapernick, Kal stated, "In a bad way, it shows how divisive a lot of people still are. I think a lot of White people just want to just be like, 'Guys, it was years ago. Let's get over this kind of thing.'" The individuals Kal described are minimizing the institutionally racist practices people of color face daily by encouraging them to "get over it." Cata and Arthur also used this frame to differentiate between ignorance and racism. Arthur stated:

> It took me a while to realize the difference between racism and ignorance... Initially, to me, anytime somebody disagrees with or treats anybody differently or thinks anything differently, like, "Oh, you are Hispanic. You must be Mexican." I'm like, "You are racist." Once I got out of Miami, because, like I said, in Miami, I feel Hispanics are very racist towards each other, but I think it's something you kind of just roll with and you deal with. We're a lot more blunt with different things. Like, I'm the darkest one in my family and they call me Negro. Like I'm Blackie. Or like you have the Asian girl in the group, they'll call her China.

Arthur used this frame in a couple of complex ways. First, he continued to stereotype Latinxs as displaying racist or prejudicial attitudes toward each other. Perhaps equally as alarming are the ways in which he minimized this racist behavior by simply advocating that individuals "just roll" and "deal" with it, arguing that it comes from ignorance rather than racism: "It's just ignorance. It's just that you haven't been exposed to it so you don't know how to react to it. It's our job as . . . And in any place you're in, as minorities . . . Like her, as a minority, I think yes, she should be correcting people. I've seen this a lot. Like, Oh, you're in a place. Now, you're the minority, but we're blaming everything on the White man. It's like, Whoa, whoa, whoa, whoa. Time out. Not all White people are the same, just like not all Black people are the same." Using ignorance as a justification for certain racial ideologies perpetuates the minimization of racism frame. Arthur went on to argue that "we're blaming everything on the White man," giving credence to the notion that the "race card" shouldn't be utilized in situations where racism is alleged and that White people aren't solely responsible for this racism. Cata further advanced this ideology:

> If we should all be together, I feel that we should all be together and we should stop blaming a color on problems and you can blame bad people on problems because there are some really scummy White people, but you know what? There are some really scummy brown people, yellow people, red people, whatever people. That's the problem. And then the more you blame it on a color and somebody having privilege or somebody having whatever . . . Like, there are a lot of poor White people, too, that don't have . . . And if you look at how they're dressed, they're not going to get the job. I think that a lot of times, like, Oh, well, that's racist, just because you didn't get the outcome you wanted. Sometimes it's not racist.

Cata's usage of this frame demonstrated its tendency to ignore structural inequalities and institutional racism, reflected in her desire to blame "bad people." Her statement here also reflected a very micro-level individualistic understanding of racism. Furthermore, she also argued against the notion of White privilege by pointing to Whites who are impoverished. Cata ended her comment by giving voice to the notion that people utilize race for personal reasons. Yet, such a statement minimizes the experiences of people of color, who must contend with the real effects of racism daily.

Darian, a forty-three-year-old male who identifies as Afro-Latino, Native American, and Puerto Rican and serves as a campus pastor, also expressed what he sees as the problematic nature of racism. He stated, "When people use that term 'racism' or 'he's racist', that to me I'm blown away by that when people go there so fast." Darian's immediate suspicion when this term is used or when someone is characterized as racist speaks to the core of this frame. He went on to say, "But to see when the officer pulls a guy over and he's harassing him, I just don't go directly to race. I go to that cop has a lot of issues. He's a jerk. And he's probably dealing with a lot of stuff at home. I think like a pastor. I think, Okay, what's that man going through? What kinds of wounds is he nursing that makes him go to harassing everyone he sees on the street? I don't go to racism first." It is important to note that Darian's interview occurred after the death of George Floyd Jr. and the protests that ensued in the wake of his death. This makes the minimization of racism on the part of Darian even more troubling.

Mavelin, a thirty-nine-year-old White and Hispanic woman who volunteers in student ministry, echoed similar sentiments: "No, I've never had horrible experiences, I've had good experiences. I've had doors opened for me, I've never had issues where I feel like I've been discriminated. Then again, that's my perspective, I see everything in sunshine. I don't take anything personal. In fact, if something happens, I'm like, Oh this person's having a bad day, that's all I think. So nothing against my race or anything like that." Both Darian and Mavelin used this frame to justify mistreatment as the result of someone having a bad day, ignoring the countless times when such incidents are in fact racially motivated.

Hans also used this frame as a tool to critique the media and describe his hesitancy to use the racism label:

> I haven't personally looked at data that breaks down number of people who are shot by police who are unarmed and their racial background. So I can't speak on whether that is or is not something. I do think that media runs on sensationalized coverage. And again, media outlets, the more people who watch, the more people who click, the more money they make. And so, which to be honest, I don't think that's a bad thing. It's a free enterprise system, which I'm not opposed to . . . Why is it that every time a twister goes through the Midwest, the cameras are always at the mobile home park? Because that's where the worst devastation happens, and so they highlight that. Sometimes I feel like it makes it seem like things are worse than they actually are . . . I haven't studied it enough to feel comfortable calling it racism.

Rather than acknowledge America's racial past or the possibility that institutional racism plays a part in the interactions between unarmed Black people and police, Hans minimized racism by shifting responsibility to the media for the ways in which these incidents are covered. Despite their pervasiveness, Hans admitted he doesn't feel comfortable calling these events racist. His use of this frame exemplifies its effect of relieving the dominant group of responsibility for the effects and outcomes of racism.

The Style of Colorblindness

Bonilla-Silva (2018, 77) defined the style of an ideology as anything from "its peculiar linguistic manners and rhetorical strategies (or race talk), to the technical tools that allow users to articulate its frames and story lines." Style emerges through what Bonilla-Silva called slippery, contradictory, and subtle forms of color-blind language. Specifically, he described five stylistic components of colorblindness: Whites' avoidance of direct racial language, semantic moves, projection, diminutives, and rhetorical incoherence. These styles became more salient following the civil rights era where speaking negatively about race and racism publicly became socially unacceptable and reflect Whites' efforts to talk about race without necessarily talking about it. In what follows, we discuss the appearance of these styles in the data from our case study.

AVOIDANCE OF DIRECT RACIAL LANGUAGE

According to Bonilla-Silva (2018), the avoidance of direct racial language on the part of Whites when expressing racial views manifests as talking in a "very careful, indirect, hesitant manner and occasionally, even through coded language." Examples of this style include comments such as "I'm not comfortable with certain types of people" or "I don't really go to that side of town."

Cata and Arthur's language exemplified this style when, during their interview, they detailed their concerns about driving through certain parts of a south Florida city:

> CATA: You know how downtown is.
> ARTHUR: And downtown, I think overall, things have been shifting a lot. They've tried to clean downtown a lot, but especially growing up in Clarkstown. There's parts of Clarkstown that they're cleaning, parts of Wileyville that are beautiful, but growing up in Clarkstown, you kind of grow up with that, "Oh, wait. Wileyville. No, don't go in Wileyville. Don't go into Midtown." So, it's little things that at night I'm like, "You're driving through Midtown at night? Okay." I definitely would worry.

Without mentioning race, Arthur describes his hesitancy about going through certain neighborhoods, all of which are predominantly Black. His justification for not going to these areas is not based on his own experiences but reflects what he heard about these neighborhoods while growing up. He avoids direct racial language by not directly stating that these communities are predominantly Black; however, the implications of his statement are that these predominantly Black areas are unsafe and should be avoided. He also avoids direct racial language when referring to these neighborhoods as being cleaned, which is often coded language for Whitening or gentrification.

PROJECTION

Bonilla-Silva (2018) described projection as a tool we use to defend ourselves and create a corporate identity, noting that "projection helps all of us 'escape from guilt and responsibility and affix blame elsewhere'" (87). Those who utilize this frame project racism onto Blacks and other persons of color as a method to avoid personal responsibility. Examples of this include "They are the racist ones, not me" or saying "I think they segregate themselves" when referring to a group of minorities in a social setting.

In our research, we found this style employed by actors associated with WWC For instance, as already discussed, Alyssa, when using the cultural racism frame, projected discrimination onto Latinxs. Similarly, when Cata used the cultural racism frame to describe Cubans, she projected racism on to them. Chris Fells, for his part, stated that "I would say this, and it's probably not a popular opinion that people would probably hold, but I share this with my boy who, he's my nephew and we're fostering to adopt, but he's Black and Samoan. And I told Joshua, 'Joshua, you need to understand this, that all of us are racist to a certain degree because it's our sinful nature.'" Chris used two styles here: semantic move and projection. In describing the conversation with his nephew, Chris essentially stated that everyone is complicit in racism. Although projection places responsibility on others, especially minorities, Chris projected this not only onto his Black/Samoan nephew but also on himself. This may still be considered a projection because including oneself as culpable in the perpetuation of racism along with everyone else, one feels less responsible. Essentially, it is difficult to feel bad or burden the shoulder of blame for something everyone else is also guilty of doing.

DIMINUTIVES

Diminutives are a stylistic component of colorblindness that seeks to "soften" racial blows (Bonilla-Silva 2018), used to maintain a color-blind form of communication that appears nonracist. For example, instead of saying "I am against affirmative action," one might say "I am just a little bit against affirmative action." Or, when speaking about interracial marriage, an individual might say, "I am just a bit concerned about the welfare of the children." This style encompasses the idea of partial or accidental racism. Moule (2009, 321) defined unintentional racism as "racism that is usually invisible even *and especially* to those who perpetrate it." Most people do not want to be considered racists because "good people do not discriminate or in any way participate in racism" (Dovidio and Gaertner 2005, 2) and yet unintentional racism persists, often rooted in stereotypes and prejudices.

This unintentionality emerged among several interviewees through the use of diminutive style. The rationale seems to be that if racism is not intentional, then it is not racism. For example, Hans used this style to describe what he refers to as "accidental" racism: "Now, after living here and understanding some of these different cultural nuances and that, I've kind of developed a subset to racism that I just refer to as accidental racism, when you simply don't know what you don't know. You don't know that something is offensive to a person, or a people group. Whether it's something that you laugh at, or things like that, where you, like I said before, where you accidentally end up offending people." Because his racism is unintended, in his view it is "accidental" and therefore not as bad as intentional racism. This view lacks an understanding of institutional racism, in which the dominant group often passively reproduces racism.

In another example, Kal used this style when responding to a question asking if the election of Barack Obama signaled that race does not matter and racism could no longer be used as an excuse for lack of success in society. Kal admitted that the eight years of the Obama presidency did not ensure equity for all; however, he recognized that some might have taken Obama's election as a sign that racism is over. He stated, "I feel like, it just gives people who are racist, and even if they don't feel like they're racist, they're a little bit racist, to be like, 'No but you've had your Black president. We're good now. We're even.'" Kal used a diminutive to describe this group as a "little bit" racist, to soften his own criticism of their racialized ideology.

Darian also used this style to refer to what he considers to be "subconscious" racism. Specifically, "When I hear a man say racial derogatory, direct overt racial comments then he's racist. This is racism. But when I hear people say dumb sort Freudian slip, not conscious like sort of subconscious racism . . . But can I say he's racist? I don't know. That's hard to tell." Although Darian was not referring to himself, he did avoid blaming individuals for racism if he perceives its manifestation to be subconscious or unintentional. Yet, as Bonilla-Silva (2018) reminds us, colorblindness has become the dominant ideology because of its slippery nature, which can come across as unintentional; this does not, however, negate its inherent racist qualities.

RHETORICAL INCOHERENCE

Rhetorical incoherence describes the process by which one becomes almost incomprehensible while discussing sensitive matters, particularly racial topics. Rhetorical incoherence includes grammatical mistakes, lengthy pauses, and repetition. Although a part of speech in general, it emerges particularly strongly when Whites discuss race. Per Bonilla-Silva (2018), this is not technically a style of colorblind racism; however, due to its prevalent usage, he included it in discussing these styles.

When discussing staff diversity, particularly the diversity of the ALT, Grace slipped into rhetorical incoherence. She said, "I think it's pretty diverse. Do I think it could be more diverse? Yeah. I think that I would love to see, in the future, if the Lord would grant us someone of color, I think that that would be special. But in and of itself, I think that there is diversity there. They're not all the same." Although Grace acknowledged that there is diversity within the ALT by beginning and ending her statements referencing this diversity, in the middle of this acknowledgment, she seemed to stutter and become muddled in expressing her desire for a person of color to be added to this group. Furthermore, the reference to "someone of color" is interesting because she acknowledged prior to this quote that there are people of color, including an Asian and Latinxs, already serving on the ALT. She seemed to be signaling that she would like to see a Black person added; however, her inability to explicitly name this contributed to the incoherence of the statement.

Similarly, Hojuma exhibited rhetorical incoherence when reflecting on the diversity of church leadership. She stated, "Although, we have Spanish services, services in Spanish, but a lot of times when they call the church or something, they want to talk to somebody who speaks Spanish, I'm sure. I'm not there, so I don't know that, but yeah." This quote in fact combines a diminutive style and rhetorical incoherence. Specifically, she stated her belief that when Spanish-speaking individuals call the church they want to speak to someone in their primary language; however, she ends by stating, "I'm not there, so I don't know." Incomprehensibly, she simultaneously states her viewpoint and discounts it.

Leaders and Volunteers/Members

Before concluding this chapter, we find it critical to discuss positionality in the church and its impact. The race and racism literature suggests that individuals and groups with resources or higher status tend to have the greatest impact in terms of messaging (Blumer 1958; Bonilla-Silva 2018; Carter and Lippard 2020).

As it relates to WWC, the views of leaders undoubtedly have a broader impact and affect the views of members in the church. However, from our experience with the church, we argue that the leaders of WWC not only have the power to shape views and perspectives of WWC members but also reflect the views and values of the congregation. That is to say, the leaders feel the weight of and may feel the need to reflect the views of the congregation. Leaders take responsibility for cohesion and group unity. As will be noted in later chapters, the aversion to preaching sermons on race and inequality is grounded in the desire to not "harm" or offend any member of the WWC community. As can be seen in our descriptions of interview participants, we take great care in describing their individual roles; however, whether they serve as a volunteer or staff leader, their responses reflect the WWC culture, a culture carefully crafted, balanced, and maintained by both leaders and members.

Conclusion

According to some scholars, including Eduardo Bonilla-Silva (2018), in the wake of the civil rights advancements of the 1960s, colorblindness has become the dominant racial ideology, transforming the ways in which people think, talk, and "do" race. This dominant racial ideology reflects and defends the racial structure that places Whites at the top (dominant group) and Blacks (subordinate group) at the bottom. The ways in which predominantly Whites use this racial ideology can be both active and passive, reproducing it in seemingly innocent ways and in minority majority spaces. Furthermore, colorblindness serves as the framework for reproduction and contestation, leading to the development of counterframes often used by the subordinate group to challenge the dominant racial ideology. These counterframes will be explored in the next chapter.

Bonilla-Silva (2018) posed that the reproduction of colorblindness as the dominant racial ideology is characterized by four primary frames: abstract liberalism, naturalization, cultural racism, and minimization of racism. These frames form the core of colorblindness and provide the road map for its utilization. In addition to the frames of colorblindness, Bonilla-Silva (2018) also described the style of colorblindness, which includes avoidance of direct racial language, semantic moves, projection, diminutives, and rhetorical incoherence. The style of colorblindness describes how those frames are used to talk about race.

All frames were utilized by leaders and members of WWC, particularly the frames naturalization and cultural racism. Perhaps the usage of the naturalization frame was popular because interview respondents used it to describe why they believe racially homogenous organizations, particularly churches, are not racist, specifically with regards to the racial makeup of several of the locations of WWC. Moreover, this frame was also utilized to justify why a Black pastor could not lead a predominantly Hispanic campus in a predominantly Hispanic community.

Although the contact hypothesis theory suggests that cross-racial contact should foster more progressive racial attitudes, perhaps it is precisely this cross-racial contact that makes members of the community feel more comfortable utilizing these frames. Being in a multiracial space and forming relationships with others of differing races allows one to feel more comfortable appealing to certain stereotypes, especially if members of those groups promote said stereotypes. Participation in a multiracial space allows one to seem nonracist while utilizing racist frames. While there are fewer examples, most of the components of the style of colorblindness were also utilized by members of wwc to "soften" or even avoid the use of direct racial language. Even in a multiracial community, all its members including people of color, utilized the frames and styles of colorblindness in ways that tangibly denied opportunities to Blacks and preserved the racial structure.

While Bonilla-Silva provided four key frames in color-blind ideology, he never stated that other frames are not used by Whites and non-Whites when it comes to racial issues. The next chapter describes how church members and leaders used other more socio-theological color-blind frames to minimize issues of race and racism that persist in society as well as to oppose efforts seeking social justice within and outside the church. As will be seen, such framing techniques fit neatly with religious teachings and practices.

CHAPTER 3

Social Justice, Socio-Theological Color-Blind Frames, and the Reproduction of Racism

Reflections from the First Author

My Emmett Till. The death of Trayvon Martin in 2012 was an inflection point in my personal development, the way in which I understood race, and my commitment to social activism. His death served as a catalyst, sparking much needed conversation, birthing the BLM movement, and revealing that though the country had a Black president, these kinds of racialized events were still very real. Since then, similar tragedies, especially officer-involved shootings, have gripped the consciousness of America.

Often, when events of this kind take place, faith leaders from around the country and world offer their prayers, praying for the victim as well as the perpetrators. I realize that praying is easy. Prayers can be nonpolitical. Prayers don't cause tension. Prayers don't alienate.

Personally, I found so much solace and comfort in the social movement that erupted around the world after the murder of George Floyd Jr. Finally, a cross-section of America—including people from every race, ethnicity, religion, class, and orientation—decided to turn its prayers into direct action. As a result, systems were shaken, and organizations were changed for the better.

Introduction

In the previous chapter, we examined how leaders and members of WWC used color-blind frames when discussing racialized issues. We found that these individuals indeed employed each of the four types of color-blind frames described by Bonilla-Silva (2018): abstract liberalism, naturalization, cultural racism, and minimization of racism. When discussing issues of a racial nature, church members and leaders often attributed inequality to individual choices while omitting any discussion of systemic racism and discrimination (abstract liberalism), justified a lack of diversity as a natural consequence of racial differences while ignoring historical causes of racial segregation (naturalization), concluded that certain groups were prone to racism (cultural racism), and propagated the idea that certain groups need to get over themselves because not all acts perceived as such are in fact racist (minimization of racism). While this may seem innocuous to the casual observer, it is clear to us that these frames were used by members and leaders of WWC to minimize problems facing Black citizens and other marginalized groups. It is also clear that these frames restricted WWC from engaging in conversations and advocacy around racial justice. While this would have been unsurprising in the context of predominantly White churches, it was disconcerting to find it to be true of this multiracial congregation. Our findings thus also support the growing body of research raising concerns about the racial liberalizing effect of multiracial churches (Edwards 2008a, 2008b, 2014; Okuwobi 2018; Oyakawa 2019).

According to Bonilla-Silva (2018), such attempts to wipe away or at least minimize historical and contemporary issues facing Black Americans and other marginalized groups have disastrous consequences because they prop up a system of oppression even as they are packaged in a seemingly benign fashion. He described such framing as "racism lite" because it lacks the brutality and harshness of traditional racism frames that attributed racial differences to biological and/or cultural inferiority relative to their White counterparts. Despite the seemingly neutral packaging, Bonilla-Silva (2018) asserted that the outcome is ultimately the same: marginalized groups are blamed for their plight, allowing for the maintenance and even flourishing of a racialized system that benefits Whites at their expense.

However, Bonilla-Silva never claimed that the four frames he outlined were the only ideological frames used to prop up a racialized system. In what follows, we show that in the case of WWC other frames, which take on both color-blind and socio-theological characteristics, are used by the church members and leaders to dismiss discussion of critical issues of race, discrimination, and racial justice. This chapter specifically seeks to extend the work of Assata Zerai (2011) by revealing the existence of color-blind frames in addition to those discussed by Bonilla-

Silva, as well as extending the counterframe of social justice. As will be seen, the frames we discuss are noteworthy because they use religious scripture and teachings to minimize racial issues facing marginalized groups and dismiss movements striving for social justice.

In her work, Zerai (2011) connected the usage of colorblindness, the subordination of race-talk, and the nonpursuit of social justice in multiracial churches. She examined three congregations, one of which she described as a predominantly African American church and two multiracial congregations. Of the three churches, sites 1 and 3 explicitly combatted colorblindness by advocating for Black liberation theology and intersectionality with a focus on the eradication of racism, sexism, classism, and heterosexism. These congregations also implemented social justice strategies aimed at eliminating these forms of domination. Conversely, Zerai found that site 2, a multiracial congregation located in a college town, practiced colorblindness by not having a focus on social change, not acknowledging racism or homogenous leadership, and not creating a space for Whites to understand the experiences and views of Black congregants.

For Zerai, the social-justice-oriented nature of sites 1 and 3 are emblematic of the countercultures described by Bonilla-Silva (2003, 77). Specifically, he noted that "Blacks have historically internalized White supremacist standards . . . (and) . . . stereotypes developed by Whites about Blacks, nevertheless, groups subordinated along racial, class or gender lines develop oppositional views . . . and even counter cultures." In his view, these countercultures were formed in opposition to the dominant racial ideology and provide an opportunity for real social change: "When the counter views of oppressed groups match periods of deep sociopolitical crisis and social upheaval, they can produce fundamental breaks and even revolutionary transformations in the social structure" (77). For many, this described the period after the death of George Floyd Jr. on May 25, 2020, when millions flocked to the streets amid a pandemic to express their outrage over his murder. The social justice counterframe espoused by the many movements for Black lives across the country coincided with public outcry, producing an opportunity for transformative societal change.

Turning back to Zerai specifically, her research led her to conclude (2011, 269) that "unless multiracial congregations are actively involved in dismantling the racial hierarchy of the U.S., they are practicing color-blind racism." For Zerai dismantling racism and adopting an anti-color-blind approach involved acknowledging racism (including color-blind racism) in all U.S. institutions and beginning to work toward a unified vision of what it means to build God's kingdom on earth. She also recommended that multiracial congregations dismantle not only racism but also sexism, ableism, heterosexism, and classism, all aspects of what Patricia Hill Collins (1990, 2000) labeled the matrix of domination.

Zerai (2011, 269) went on to say, "If these aspects of American society are not addressed, the implicit (and sometimes explicit) expectation of majority members (Whites, those who enjoy racial privilege in this society), is that marginalized folk will 'go with the flow.'" She concluded that multiracial churches should become a base for social protest and a new civil rights movement that would work to extend the benefits of American citizenship to all Americans. Following Zerai, unless multiracial congregations are engaged in the work of social justice, which includes the acknowledgment and active dismantling of racism, they are perpetuating colorblindness, the dominant racial ideology.

What does this mean for wwc? This chapter extends Zerai's findings, as we examine wwc's understanding, framing, and pursuit (or lack thereof) of social justice. First, we explore the various understandings of social justice and then examine the ways in which wwc members and leaders understand social justice, asking whether these understandings conflict with colorblindness or perpetuate colorblindness. Furthermore, we explore other frames with a color-blind slant that emerged out of the data. These frames, which we have termed "socio-theological," represent a synthesis of both sociological and theological concepts. They work to minimize and contest the social justice counterframe by making use of religious texts and other church teachings to minimize persistent problems of systemic racism and discrimination, thereby perpetuating the dominant racial ideology.

Data for this analysis come from interviews of multiracial leaders and members of the church as well as from a close reading of church social media posts. While the interviews provide a sense of the church norms on these topics, the social media posts shed some light on the formal stances of the church.

Social Justice

Though used far and wide, the term "social justice" often remains vague and undefined. According to David Miller (1976, 20) justice is "the manner in which benefits and burdens are distributed among men (strictly, sentient beings) whose qualities and relationships can be investigated." In a just society, these benefits and burdens are distributed based on what Miller (1976, 20) described as "personal characteristics and circumstances." It is important to note that Miller (1976) distinguished justice from social justice, which he defined as "the distribution of benefits and burdens throughout a society, as it results from the major social institutions—property systems, public organizations, etc." (22).

According to Tyler et al. (1997), the field of social justice research can be divided into four waves from 1945 to the present. The first wave established the basic understanding that satisfaction and dissatisfaction with the distribution of goods and services are linked to comparisons between what people have and what they feel they deserve. The second wave focused on distributive justice and found that people ultimately care about justice and shape their feelings and actions according to what they believe is fair or unfair. This wave also explored the concept of equity and found that people judge a situation to be fair if their ratio of inputs to outcomes is comparable to that of others. The third wave focused on procedural justice, examining the fairness of different ways of resolving conflicts. The fourth wave is ongoing and explores the notion of retributive justice, finding that the American public has become increasingly concerned about rule breaking, especially in the context of the criminal justice system.

It can be argued that our understanding of *social justice* may become clearer in the face of a *social injustice*, for example, the murder of George Floyd Jr. The recognition of injustice often produces an uncomfortable and distressing emotional state (Adams 1965; Austin and Walster 1980), which motivates people to advocate for the restoration of justice. In the case of Floyd, this can be seen in the demonstrations, sit-ins, and even violent looting in response to his death. These responses were a clear reaction not only to the manner in which Floyd died at the hands (or knee) of Derek Chauvin but also to the history of police brutality endured by Black Americans and other marginalized members of society.

Tyler and Smith (1995) have argued that social injustices reveal two types of groups: the advantaged and the disadvantaged. The advantaged seek to protect the racial and social order by engaging in psychological strategies that avoid taking responsibility for compensation and restitution to the harmed (Lerner 1981; Mikula 1986; Taylor and Moghaddam 1994), protect positive self-image, and distort the norms of distributive justice. For their part, although the recent movement for Black lives has encompassed a wide range of people, the social justice literature finds that the disadvantaged often do not act in the face of injustice (Major 1994; Martin 1986; Wright, Taylor and Moghaddam 1990), which may be attributed to a sense of powerlessness. Furthermore, Tyler and Smith (1995) argued that the outrage of the disadvantaged may not manifest into action because they have become accustomed to their situation or feel as if the injustice may not be legitimated by those in privileged positions. The disadvantaged may also deny that they are the personal victims of injustice because doing so means accepting a victimized position, which could cause damage to one's self-esteem and sense of control over the world (Bulman and Wortman 1977; Mikula 1993); it could also require victims to identify perpetrators, which could prove costly emotionally (Crosby and Gonzalez-Intal 1984; Montada 1991).

The various tensions arising from one's positionality as advantaged or disadvantaged play a major role in the acknowledgement of injustice. Exploring these tensions can clarify WWC's delayed decision to respond to Floyd's death and the church's silence in response to other social injustices. More concretely, the response to injustice may depend upon: (1) practical concerns, such as the likelihood of success/retaliation; (2) the ambiguity of the situation; (3) whether the procedures or situation producing the injustice are perceived as legitimate; and (4) the relationship of both the victim and perpetrator to the larger collective (Tyler and Smith 1995). Moreover, the perceived cost of harm plays a big role in whether those who commit the injustice seek to rectify it. Notably, those responsible for injustices are more likely to attempt to restore equity if they can do so completely (Walster, Walster, and Berscheid 1978).

Injustices that cause the loss of life are more complicated in that life cannot be compensated for. Still, although cursory, this exploration of social justice provides context for exploring how social justice is framed at WWC. We contend that when utilized, social justice can be a powerful counterframe to colorblindness. Its absence may speak to the proliferation of colorblindness, the dominant racial ideology in the United States. The next section examines socio-theological color-blind frames that emerged from our interviews with church members and leaders. Often, members used frames that conflicted with and even sought to minimize the counterframe of social justice; we found that here these frames served as psychological tools to justify and maintain the racial order. As we noted earlier, this pattern has been mostly associated with White churches, which some scholars claim function as key players in a racialized social system because they reproduce racial ideology and ignore systemic issues of racism and discrimination (Jones 2021). It is thus all the more important notable that we have found it to be true of the multiracial context of our case study.

Multiracial Churches: What about Institutional Racism Perspectives?

The literature describing the implications of institutional (or systemic) racism is abundant (Miller and Garran 2007) and reveals that institutional racism impacts all institutions and every facet of American life, including housing and neighborhoods; education; employment; wages, wealth accumulation and upward mobility; the environment; health; the criminal justice system; and religion (Carter and Lippard 2020). Indeed, Bonilla-Silva (2018) pointed out that anyone who seeks to ignore the persistent impact of race and racism on our social world has to do major mental gymnastics and ignore a vast literature that addresses these problems. In other words, those who refuse to acknowledge the racialized social world we live in are living in a fantasy land that props up a system that benefits Whites at the expense of Black folks and other marginalized groups.

As mentioned earlier, one supposed positive characteristic of going to a multiracial church is that members interact with others from different social backgrounds. In doing so, members become well aware of challenges facing others of different races related to systemic racism and discrimination and can then challenge their own views on race. We found that some members of WWC did indeed acknowledge broader systemic issues. For example, when asked if the election of Barack Obama signaled that racism is a thing of the past, members acknowledged both racism and systemic racism. For example, Kal, a White campus ministry leader introduced in an earlier chapter, stated, "So, no, having a Black president once for eight years does not completely get rid of the systemic problems and issues that have come from and been birthed from all the oppression and everything that happened from beforehand." Although Kal did not refer to racism directly, it was understood that he was referring to systemic racism, considering the question dealt with the topic of race and racism. He went on to say, "I see their names. I see their faces. I know their stories. I know their lives. I see even the issues that have come up, with the systemic problem that we have with racial inequality."

Other church members held this perspective as well. Chris Fells, one of the campus pastors, acknowledged systemic racism and prejudice in passing when describing what he sees as the major inequality facing Black communities, the absence of fathers. He said, "I think the biggest injustice to the impoverished community, or say the community I grew up in or the Black community, if you will, would be a lack of a father-figure before anything else." When asked how the death of George Floyd Jr. was framed by WWC, Mac, a leader who oversees one of the ministries for all the campuses, responded by saying, "We framed it in student ministry, as you probably saw, the systemic racism issue." Moreover, when asked if organizations can be racist, Jake, a White volunteer, responded, "So if an organization, now it might not be their own fault, and it may be, but that organization is in a predominantly White area or on the other spectrum a predominantly Black area, and it's a predominantly Black organization or White, there could be systemic racism underlying that they don't realize just because people groups like to be together with their people." These examples all acknowledge to varying degrees that systemic racism exists and is a tangible concept for these individuals.

Perhaps it was Joe, a White male campus leader who identifies as Cuban, who provided the most nuanced understanding of systemic racism. He argued that there are south Florida Latinx people who have been negatively impacted by systemic racism; however, because they have been able to build wealth, they minimize racism and its implications for others:

> And then we've still got systemic racism flowing throughout this country ... So when they look at systemic racism, they don't think that it exists primarily because, "Hey look, here we've made it work. Why can't the rest of the country be like here?" Because they don't have the same opportunities over there. "Oh, but that's their fault. They're not working hard" ... So even an understanding of the justice system and how it holds people back in terms of systemic racism, in terms of, "Hey, so so-and-so got arrested just for being in the wrong place in the wrong part of the city on a Friday night. He couldn't afford bail and so now he's stuck in jail. And then he was released, but he's got to pay all these fees and all this stuff, so he can't go to school and he can't do this." "Oh well, it's his fault for being in the wrong [of town." We just acknowledged that he was falsely arrested. "Doesn't matter, if he were smarter, he wouldn't have been here."

Joe not only described the minimization of racism frame but also highlighted the real consequences of institutional and systemic racism especially when describing the effects of being arrested on the economically marginalized. These examples make clear that members of WWC understood, to some degree, the implications of racism, an important component of what Zerai (2011) described as the work of multiracial congregations. However, this acknowledgment is contradicted by another color-blind frame we termed socio-theologizing of racism, which occurs when individuals use Scripture and/or other teachings to minimize racism or its effects.

Socio-Theological Color-Blind Frames and the Minimization of Social Justice

From the interviews, it was clear that WWC members made use of frames that borrowed from theological teachings and Scripture to actively minimize issues dealing with race, racism, and social activism. The synthesis of sociological and theological frameworks resembles the established subdiscipline known as the sociology of religion, which can be defined as the intersectionality of societies and religion, studying how "religious factors penetrate the process of creating society, the role religion plays in the constitution of social groups, and the influence religious values and norms exert on people's behavior and their interpretation of everyday life" (Szymczak 2020, 512).

While this synthesis seems commonsense and natural, especially as it relates to the ways in which groups within society use theological teachings as guideposts to interact with each other, scholars have pointed out some weaknesses of a socio-theological framework. For example, Hughes (2017) points out the potential of theologians to be ignorant of sociological concepts and methods as well as the risk that sociologists will not take seriously issues of faith and religion he sees as critical to human existence. While no interdisciplinary approach is free of challenges, we felt the term "socio-theological" aptly describes the ways in which these frames garnered from our data are grounded within a theological paradigm, with consequences for how adherents understand society, inequalities, social movements, and social justice.

THE THEOLOGIZING RACISM AS A SIN FRAME

The "theologizing racism as a sin" frame was primarily evident when it came to the labeling of racism as "sin." This idea of "sin" and how it relates to everyday life for church members at wwc and in general is a key component of theology and church teachings. The "original sin" as described in Genesis 3 relates to what Christians believe is humanity's first transgression against God, consequently allowing sin to enter the world. For Christians, sin is not only a violation of God's laws, it also represents a disruption in the relationship between God and humanity. The results of this disruption include everything from acts of violence, injustices, relationship failures, diseases, and ultimately death.

Christians believe that Christ's death and resurrection represents power over sin; the victory is not yet complete, however, as only Christ's return will definitively end sin and assure the perfection of humanity. These theological teachings are cited throughout Scripture and are held sacred by many Christians, including evangelicals generally and members of wwc specifically. Manifestly, in Christian teachings, being absolved of sin requires repentance and forgiveness by God through Christ's sacrifice. Implicitly, this allows for social control in that the consequences of sin, for example social injustices, may not be addressed directly because of the belief that the root cause of these injustices is first and foremost spiritual in nature.

Unsurprisingly, sin as a controlling mechanism was readily apparent in interviews we conducted and other sources of data, especially when discussing issues of a racialized nature. We argue that the consequences of this language perpetuate the idea that since racism is a sin, its dismantling is not to be found in humanity or social justice efforts; rather, the solution is found in Jesus Christ. The consequence of such framing is detrimental for those seeking racial progress and change. That is to say, the dismantling of racism through the counterframe of social justice is minimized by this color-blind, socio-theological frame, which emphasizes the universal nature of human sin and rejects the notion that social justice should be pursued. For example Cata, a White female ministry leader we've encountered before, stated, "We're all sinners and I believe that we are not going to get everything perfect until Jesus comes back and makes the world perfect, to be honest with you . . . There's no light without Christ. And so, I feel that in the same way, you're going to be in desperation and alcoholism. You're going to be in desperation in your sexual sin. Like, imagine outside of that. So, think that racism, it's another level of sinful yuck." Cata's statement here reveals the color-blind nature of this socio-theological frame in a few ways. First, she notes that everyone is a sinner, and no one can become "perfect" until Jesus returns. Furthermore, she likens racism to alcoholism and sexual sin, contradicting findings that racism is a learned behavior (Bell 2004), as opposed to alcoholism and perhaps sexual addictions, which may be linked to biological and genetic factors (Potenza 2013). Finally, she never advocates for a path that directly confronts racism, suggesting she believes that it is ultimately the responsibility of an all-powerful deity to eliminate such issues.

Another example of this can be seen in a statement made by Mike, a Puerto Rican campus pastor: "And the Bible says He just died on the cross for the sins of men, not White men, or Black men, or whatever." Grace, a White woman, also used this frame to contextualize racism as sin, stating, "Personally, I think it's kind of a generational sin. I consider racism a sin . . . However, they have spoken on race and racism, how it's a sin . . . but I can remember times where it's been brought up, like as an illustration, or it's been called out as a sin, as part of a sermon . . . Also exposing the truth of what racism is, which is, it's a sin." Grace, like others, theologized racism and suggested that it can be passed down, like a genetic trait. As we spoke with her, she reflected on the history of WWC. In addition to saying that racism had not been discussed very much within the organization over time, she noted that when it *was* mentioned it was also framed as sin. This color-blind theology emphasizes the oneness of all people, essentializes the actions of Jesus, and minimizes social justice efforts, rendering them futile in comparison to the power of God. The idea that sin impacts all can be extended to color-blind propagandists who argue that reverse racism exists or that Whites are not the main perpetuators of the dominant racial ideology.

Indeed, the idea that racism is a sin makes the problems facing Black folks and other people of color more of an individual issue rather than one rooted in systemic and historical relations. For example, another WWC campus pastor, Darian, told us, "race is a heart issue. Yes, the Gospel is the only thing that changes the heart of man." Two aspects of this comment are apparent. One, similar to the examples already discussed, Darian believes that only an all-powerful deity can eliminate the issues of race and discrimination facing our society. Two, this comment reveals that the issue of sin is reduced to an individual level construct, thus absolving organizations and institutions that reproduce racial inequality through discriminatory rules and practices (Ray 2019).

In response to the death of George Floyd Jr., WWC made a social media post four days later. The post was composed of the following words: "Every person is created in the image of God. Racism is destructive. We mourn with those who weep. We pray for change. We rest in the perfect judgment of God." The implications of this post will be described in detail later in this chapter; here, we want to address one of the comments made in response to it. Specifically, this comment furthers the notion that racism is a sin as well as the idea that God is ultimately responsible for its eradication; thus, minimizing any pursuits for social justice through color-blind socio-theological appeals. A comment on Instagram by a member of the WWC community, stated:

> Truly saddened by the news of #georgefloyd. #Racism is a symptom of the sin problem. It's tragic. WE (every color of us) are made in the image of God but I'm still left wondering why we always seem to seek out someone or something to be against. #COVID19 gave the world a common enemy and for a brief moment the world seemed to get along as we fought against the #virus. Sadly this news reminds me that #violence will not cease until Jesus makes it cease. Prayers for the Floyd family. Prayers for the 99.9% of #officers whose good name is tarnished because of the wickedness of a few. #Prayers for those few to come to repent of their sin. 🙏 🙏 🙏 🙏 🙏 🙏 🙏 🙏 🙏 🙏 🙏 🙏

This user directly attributed racism to sin, promoted colorblindness, argued that the end of violence will occur upon the return of Jesus Christ, offered prayers for officers, and encouraged others to repent. Although the commentator acknowledged the existence of racism, the social justice counterframe was again minimized by a color-blind theology that makes God the sole arm and arbiter of justice.

The church's social media postings thereafter advertised a "Pastoral Conversation" on racial injustice. These posts included the following words: "Listen in on a conversation with our teaching team on racial injustice . . . Together we'll learn how to navigate the sin of racism through the lens of the gospel." Although the discussion of racial injustice in this forum begins to acknowledge systemic racism, it is framed as a sin which again carries the implication that only a divine force has the power to eliminate it.

This conversation was led by the church's teaching team, which included the lead pastor, the pastor emeritus, the associate teaching pastor, and Pastor Matthew, the only African American member of this group. Pastor Matthew led much of the discussion and began by providing a biblical foundation for the argument that racism is sin. Claiming that "the divisions of race is really the result of sin," he went on to say that "the complete redemption of mankind . . . will result in the complete defeat of racism." Pastor Matthew added that the task of humanity is to work to make earth like heaven; however, he provided no further discussion or understanding of what that looks like. From a social justice perspective, it seems this discussion should have been an opportunity for social justice to be inserted into the conversation as a counterframe. To us, this demonstrated the scope of the color-blind ideology in general and color-blind frames in particular.

In conclusion, a great deal of the discussion among members and with this teaching team followed a predictable logic: (1) acknowledge racism; (2) frame racism as sin; and (3) reference a color-blind theology with Jesus as the central figure, who upon His return will eradicate racism. The implications of this framing technique are disastrous for progress. Perhaps the most consequential outcome is that it minimizes the social justice counterframe, portraying human attempts to achieve social justice as futile. This was never more evident than after the murder of George Floyd Jr., where the Black Lives Matter movement and other organizations seeking change had significant momentum and support. The effects of this can be seen in the next socio-theological frame we discuss here, theologizing justice.

THE THEOLOGIZING JUSTICE FRAME—"ONE DAY BUT NOT TODAY"

To recall, Zerai argued that unless multiracial churches adopt a social justice counterframe, they are practicing color-blind racism and not helping to end racial inequality. This idea is central to the work of Bonilla-Silva and other scholars who link a lack of acknowledgement to the reproduction of inequality. For example, Carter and Lippard (2020) posed that, even among supporters of affirmative action, the lack of acknowledgment of past and contemporary racism is detrimental to the continued fight against inequality and oppression. They found that both opponents and supporters of affirmative action produced arguments completely devoid of context related to current and historical issues of racism and discrimination in society in general and in the education system in particular. Most interesting and relevant to the current study, they found supporters of affirmative action even attempted to minimize persistent racism using various frames despite the mountain of evidence to the contrary.

That said, we find WWC members and leaders made the same mistakes. They practiced colorblindness by using socio-theological frames to minimize issues surrounding race. They would often use socio-theological color-blind frames that both theologize and politicize racism and the social justice efforts that seek to redress it. When the social justice counter frame is minimized, color-blind racism remains the dominant racial ideology, hence why exploring how both racism and social justice are framed is important to understanding how racism is reproduced. Not only did interview participants theologize racism, they also used the socio-theological color-blind frame of theologizing justice, which seeks to minimize any human efforts that attempt to seek justice. For example, campus ministry leader Craig said:

> We do believe, and I believe in the Word of God and the theology that we stand on, is that nobody seeks social justice here on Earth... Listen, the Lord is a just God. He is the one at the end of the day who will seek and justify all of us. And be the one to make sure that happens. And so, it doesn't leave a gaping hole in me and there is no deeper desire here in my church, which is here to point to the Word of God... What I'm trying to say is, that when it comes down to justice, I don't believe that we're going to really attain that here. Meaning here on Earth.

For Craig, justice is in God's purview, not humanity's. Until God metes out this justice, it is the responsibility of the church to uplift biblical teachings. Here, Craig minimized social justice and perpetuated a color-blind theology with a God who justifies "all" at the center. Hojuma did so as well: "I don't think we should be there to hear a sermon about social justice stuff. I do think small groups can do that... for people who want to come... I just think when we go to church, to worship, that that should be biblical teaching and worship. And you can do biblical teaching that relates to racial issues, of course, but I don't think the focus of it should be the other." Here, Hojuma emphatically states that social justice is not something to be preached or taught on Sunday morning; rather it should be relegated to small, voluntary groups. Furthermore, issues related to race should be mentioned only when they are directly referenced within the biblical text, as opposed to centering teachings on subjects related to racial issues. Like Craig, Hojuma seemed to embrace a color-blind ideology that sought to minimize social justice teachings and efforts.

For her part, Melissa also marginalized the social justice counterframe by minimizing what can be done here on earth and focusing on what she believes will be done through God: "I'm not looking for racial justice, because again, it's not something that... I never cared about the color of my skin until I got older...

I'm not looking for racial justice because I don't think it's something we can ever perfect now." Melissa admitted that for most of her life, she subscribed to color-blindness; however, she also acknowledged that this has changed. It could very well be that the overall number of documented high-profile cases of racial injustices have caused her to become more reflexive concerning her identity and the plight of Black communities. Despite this enlightenment, she echoed Craig's belief regarding God being the arbiter of social justice, something humanity cannot ultimately effectively administer. Although the increase in media attention to the injustices Black people face has caused Melissa to become more aware of her race, the utilization of this frame is indeed problematic, as she continued to minimize actions that may ameliorate existing oppressive and marginalizing circumstances.

THE POLITICIZING RACISM AND JUSTICE FRAME

According to Michael Tesler (2016), the election of Barack Obama as president of the United States helped to usher in a "most racial" political era, in which racially liberal and conservative Americans were more divided than ever. This divide was the result of what Tesler hypothesized as the *spillover of racialization*. This hypothesis argues that a wide array of Americans' opinions—including their evaluation of Barack Obama's political rivals and allies, public policy preferences, subjective evaluations of objective economic conditions, vote choices for Congress, and partisan attachments—all became more polarized by racial attitudes during the Obama presidency.

Not only did Obama's race cause racial resentment to impact public policy preferences, but racial resentment also affected the racialized attitudes of Whites, framing everything politically connected to President Obama. Doane (2020, 28) also noted the correlation between racial ideology and politics: "Politically, groups 'weaponize' racial ideologies to attack or defend the existing racial order, for they provide the rationale for social policies and the organizing ideas for social movements." The political nature of these ideologies responds to social movements and to social and economic changes. We pose that the politicizing of racism as a social injustice and the politicizing of the response to that injustice through social justice efforts is a socio-theological, color-blind frame that emerged from the data.

To explore racial ideology and how interview participants understood racialized events, we asked them how WWC may have framed the 2016 election, the NFL protests initiated by Colin Kaepernick, the United-the-Right rally in Charlottesville, Virginia, and the May 25, 2020, death of George Floyd Jr., all of which have a racialized component. The responses to these questions were wide ranging and revealing. In several instances, interviewees politicized these events, thereby minimizing their racist nature. The story became more about the people and specific events and how politics entered the discussion and ruined what could have been gained in their aftermath. As such, members of the church minimized one of the most important aspects of these events: that the kneeling of Colin Kaepernick and the death of George Floyd Jr. could be (and were) catalysts for social justice and change in a world where these issues surrounding police brutality and overreach have too long been ignored. Nonetheless, in many cases this chance to make change and seek social justice was ignored and minimized using a color-blind ideology, which ultimately does not benefit those most in need of social justice and benefits those with the least need for change.

It is important to note that the prompt leading into these questions acknowledged the racialized nature of these events; however, for many of the interviewees, their first inclination was to deflect to a certain extent and describe the church's priority to distance itself from politics. For example, Kal a White male campus ministry leader stated, "But I've already seen that our church stays pretty far away from having a political stance." Chris, a campus pastor, similarly asserted that "We do not talk about politics here . . . I think it was in 2016, and we talked about the election, whether you vote for Hillary or Trump, whatever it may be that didn't matter . . . This is why in the past twenty-three years, and even moving forward, we'll never talk about politics. It doesn't matter if you vote Democrat, Republican or Independent . . . It doesn't matter who's in office, God is still sovereignly ruling over this nation." Both Kal and Chris echoed the sentiments of several others who observed that WWC eschewed politics. For them, politics and religion did not fit well together; as such, they seemed to say that a church does not have a responsibility toward social justice despite the history and role of the church in the civil rights movement (Calhoun-Brown 2000).

The church members provided interesting justifications for this apolitical stance. Chris argued that "political" matters are ultimately inconsequential because of the sovereign power of God. Hans, however, went into more detail as to why the church does not talk about politics: "We as a church don't want to alienate an entire . . . Most political issues are political issues because the country is split more or less 50/50, and that's why it goes back and forth on these kinds of things . . . So as a church, we don't want to alienate hypothetically half of the population that now they don't want to come to church because they disagree with the official church stance on a political issue." Hans made it clear that not only does the church avoid anything considered political but it does so in recognition of the vast political divide within the church community. To bring up politics exposes those divides and places the unity of the church at risk. Thus, and most surprisingly, the one strength of the church, that of diversity and the insights this provides as described by Zerai (2011), was now being used as a reason to *not* participate or contribute to social justice activities or conversations. This was a common tactic used by opponents of affirmative action in Carter and Lippard's (2020) study as well: affirmative action was framed as something threatening, a policy that could harm those it was supposed to help. In a seemingly cruel paternalistic twist, opponents of affirmative action sought to shut it down by arguing that those who were meant to benefit from such a policy would actually be hurt by it. Similarly, some members of WWC raised concerns that discussing and being active in the fight for social justice could be harmful to the church and its members.

This reliance on "politics" as a negative concept can also be seen in how race, racism, and social injustices are framed. For example, Craig stated, "And I think when you get into some of these social injustices, in a very public way, it becomes more of a politically charged space versus you are welcome to hear and included in what's happening here." Craig referenced social injustices in response to a question about WWC's participation in social justice activities that promote racial equality. Craig, a Black man, argued against this kind of activism because of its political ramifications. When pressed about whether the Bible would support such activities and conversations, he commented, "Absolutely. Absolutely. And I'm not saying that we shy away from them. I just think that we don't highlight them." For many of the interview participants, the Bible provided definitive answers to what societal issues are addressed and how. Although Craig believed the Bible speaks to social injustices, he also felt that the political orientation of the solutions to these injustices precluded them from being highlighted by the church. The politicizing of race, racism, and social justice minimized the church's pursuit of the social justice counterframe and created a situation whereby certain elements of the biblical text were highlighted while others were ignored for the sake of maintaining a comfortable space.

Darian both critiqued the church's involvement in social justice activities and advanced the notion that the politicization of racism and justice has caused WWC to not be involved in these efforts. He shared, "We do need to go out. We do need to be a part, more of this. It's so crummy, really. It's so crummy that sometimes we can't do it without it turning into, 'Oh, look at Without Walls turning into the Black Lives Matter movement' or 'Oh, look at Without Walls turning into Trump supporters' or whatever." Here, Daren likens BLM, a social justice-oriented movement seeking to affirm Black lives, to a political movement in support of a political figure, reinforcing the notion that racial injustice and the movements seeking to redress it are political and therefore should be avoided. Such a false equivalence results in the church ultimately not taking a strong stance against social injustice.

Mike also addressed the idea that the BLM movement is political in nature and needs to be minimized: "If our church, on Sunday morning, our pastor comes up and he says, 'I want everybody to know that we believe Black lives matter.' Unintentionally, he's making a very political statement . . . And so, I think that as a church, I would prefer and I think the safest course of action is to stay away from anything even remotely political so that we can retain integrity and be able to teach the Bible for the sake of the Bible and what it teaches, and nothing else." Mike believed advocacy for Black lives should be minimized for biblical teaching to maintain its "integrity." This continues to promote a color-blind theology and minimizes the social justice counter frame. Furthermore, he went on to comment about how it is not political for the pastor to preach a series of sermons about marriage, more specifically the traditional concept thereof, although this has been the subject of immense political debate ultimately reaching the halls of the Supreme Court. Perhaps Mike does not view this as political because it touches on an issue that is not so divisive for conservative Christians. However, such a position is problematic to race scholars because it allows for colorblindness to flourish and reduces the chances that the church will act in any manner to reduce social injustices.

Yet, this is not true of all WWC members. For example, Sydney relied on the social justice counterframe to combat the politicizing of racism and justice. She stated, "I believe racism. God talks about no favoritism. They go over the Bible racism was happening there. So, it can be preached. It can be preached there. And there are many issues that could be discussed from the pulpit. If it's in the Bible, we can talk about it. Even if we're going to use the angle of that, the pulpit is not a place for politics. I don't think racism is politics. It is something that we shouldn't do. And I know God doesn't like it, and it should be said that God doesn't like it." To recall, according to Zerai (2011), one of the components of the social justice counterframe is acknowledging the existence of racism. Unlike other interview participants, Sydney not only acknowledged racism and its place in the Bible, she also refused to frame racism as political. By doing so and by advocating that racism should be preached from the pulpit, Sydney was consciously or unconsciously fighting against colorblindness. This color-blind frame politicizing racism and social justice efforts that seek to redress it further perpetuates and reproduces color-blind racism and minimizes the social justice counterframe.

Leaders and Volunteers/Members

Again, we would like to touch on the idea that position in the church can have an impact with color-blind messages (Blumer 1958; Bonilla-Silva 2018; Carter and Lippard 2020). While it is true that leaders have the ears of the congregation during sermons, general church social events, or through the social media, we argue that, from our experience with the WWC, its leaders feel pressure to reflect the views and values of the multiracial congregation. As noted in the previous chapter, we see that the leaders take seriously the responsibility to maintain group unity in the church and feel that issues of race and racial activism may produce discord. Accordingly, these leaders develop an aversion to preaching sermons on race and inequality either out of concern for "harming" or offending any member of the WWC community or out of a desire to not bring politics into the pulpit. Thus, while their messages may have a broader range and impact than members, their views tend to succumb to what they see as the needs of the church: to be race neutral and not upset certain segments in the name of unity.

Conclusion

To further explore the reproduction of racism by WWC, we extended the work of Assata Zerai (2011), examining the proliferation of colorblindness and the contestation of the social justice counterframe. Zerai found that when the social justice counterframe is minimized, multiracial churches are practicing colorblindness. Our own research found that the social justice counterframe is minimized within the WWC through the usage of three socio-theological, color-blind frames: theologizing racism, theologizing justice, and politicizing racism and justice.

Through these socio-theological frames, members of WWC, in many instances, acknowledged racism while demonizing any attempts to dismantle it and seek opportunities for healing and justice for all. Many pointed to the potentially divisive impact of social justice efforts on the community. This is in line with previous research that found that multiracial churches primarily suit the interests of Whites (Edwards 2008a, 2008b). An emphasis on not creating divisions within the church only caters to the preferences of the dominant group and allows for the dominant ideology to go unchecked. Furthermore, for many members of this community, attempts to attain social justice are futile until God's return; therefore, social justice talk and action should be minimized and placed within the purview of God's responsibilities.

In short, our research demonstrates that WWC members use these socio-theological, color-blind frames as tools to not only promote the dominant racial ideology and maintain the racial hierarchy but to make theological justifications that appear race conscious as well. Simply praying for the victims of racial injustices allows for injustices to be recognized without any real plans or actions to ensure justice is actuated. This supposedly protects the unity of the church and allows for all political positions to remain unexamined or challenged. These practices are harmful in that the community then creates theological hierarchies in which certain subjects (that are also political landmines) like same-sex marriage are elevated, taught about, discussed, and preached about while subjects such as racial injustice (which is also evidenced in the Bible) are marginalized and even dismissed.

While White evangelical churches can openly take hostile positions due to the conflation of political, racial, and theological ideology as seen in White Christian nationalism, multiracial churches seem to foster a more flexible and fluid racial ideology that still leads its adherents to the same place: the reproduction and maintenance of racism through colorblindness. The implications of these findings are important for understanding how racism is produced and reproduced even in a multiracial space. This research essentially confirms the work of both Eduardo Bonilla-Silva (2018) and Assata Zerai (2011) by demonstrating that indeed colorblindness, whether through the frames of Bonilla-Silva or the new frames conceived from this research, provides the framework for the dominant racial ideology to proliferate and be reproduced even in a setting supposedly more racially diverse and egalitarian.

CHAPTER 4

Racialized Organizations and the Reproduction of Racism

Reflections from the First Author

I was fortunate to attend some of the greatest universities in the world. My educational journey included a top ranked historically Black college/university (HBCU), an Ivy League institution, and a state university. It also included degrees from different disciplines, from journalism to graduate theological studies, concluding with a PhD in sociology. Regardless of the discipline, there was always one commonality: the power of hard work, determination, and preparation. I was taught that if you mastered these skills, throw in a dose of good luck and/or prayers, you were all but guaranteed success.

I now know that success is a little more complicated. There are politics, timing, and other factors that impact one's career trajectory; however, race shouldn't be a negative credential for anyone seeking to advance in their career. Organizational culture and processes, all of which can be different from official policies, can cripple one's chances of advancement. In this chapter we will examine the role organizations play in the reproduction of racialized ideology and practices that impact individual life chances.

Introduction

In the previous chapters, we established that members and leaders in multiracial spaces both pull arguments and ideas from the dominant racial ideology when discussing issues of race and racism. By bringing in frames from the dominant ideology, these individuals can dismiss issues of racism and discrimination and any calls to action, ultimately maintaining the racial status quo in the church and broader society. We found that the color-blind frames outlined by Bonilla-Silva (2018) saturated both personal discussions and media posts. In an extension of this and Zerai's (2011) work on social activism, we also found that members and leaders use what we called socio-theological frames. Again, these frames are color-blind in nature, minimize talk of race and activism, but are tied directly to the scriptural teachings of the church. As such, church members and leaders even in a multiracial context produce and reproduce racial ideology that negatively impacts marginalized groups. The result is the propping up of White supremacy, the very foundation of racial inequality in our society.

In this chapter, we turn to the organizational policies and practices of wwc and assess whether they act to reinforce racial inequality. Victor Ray (2019) has developed a theoretical framework of racialized organizations, where he argues that organizations are indeed racial structures that reproduce (and even challenge) racialization processes rather than race-neutral structures. Ray poses that cognitive schemas regarding positionality (for those of high and low statuses) are connected to social and material resources through mundane daily organizational practices. The organization's distribution of these resources across racial groups allows for the dominant racial ideology (e.g., "success is produced by hard work") to become pervasive, ultimately reproducing inequality in a seemingly nonracial way.

In his theoretical framework, Ray delineates the levels of analysis at the organizational/meso level rather than the institutional/macro level or the individual/micro level. Gary Alan Fine (2012, 2) has described the meso level as the "space between individual interaction and that of large-scale organizations and institutions: not untethered behavior, but the interaction order." This includes individual workplaces, schools, and churches.

Ray focuses on the organization specifically because it serves as a vital connection between institutions (e.g., the racial state) and individual-level actors (e.g., congregants). He argues that organizations are key to the stability and change of the entire racial order in that they can magnify its power (through the distribution of social and material resources) and are the primary site of racial contestation. Focusing on the meso level allows for greater attention to and exploration of the myriad ways in which inequality is reproduced without focusing on individual attributes, like attitude or beliefs. As such, organizations serve as key forces in a racialized social system because they have a hand in the distribution of resources along racial lines, which then influences state-level processes and individual attitudes and beliefs among individuals (Ray 2019).

Ray (2019) argued that organizations are racialized and reproduce the racial status quo because they shape the agency of racial groups; legitimate the unequal distribution of resources; treat Whiteness as a credential; and decouple formal policies from informal practices in a way that benefits Whites and disadvantages other racial groups. These factors, which we discuss in greater detail, are key to producing and reproducing inequality in the organization and establishing racial schemas, the " 'taken-for-granted' mental representations generating and legitimating inequality," and resources (Ray 2019, 30).

Schemas can be understood as unwritten rule books that provide a set of "'fundamental tools of thought' for the accumulation and distribution of organizational resources" (Ray 2019, 31). Schemas are important because they account for the unequal distribution of resources—social and material—that come from seemingly race-neutral policies and practices or structures. For example, the schema of segregation was legitimated as a racial structure when enshrined in policy by the government. Accordingly, once racial structures are reified, "racial ideology—or racism—arises to justify the unequal distribution of resources along racial lines" (32), reinforcing the foundational schema.

While this chapter seeks to understand whether WWC maintains policies and practices making it a racialized organization ultimately reproducing the racial status quo, it also examines how this organization challenges the racialization processes. We will see whether the factors described by Ray appear in the data—the perspectives of church members as well organizational processes—that should tell us whether, and if so how, material and immaterial resources were distributed or constrained based on racialized ideology.

The Curious Case of Diversity

Before we go into the pillars of Ray's theory and how they play out in WWC, we would like to discuss the curious case of diversity as a guiding policy, and what it contributes to the organization. Diversity is a relevant organizational topic because it is viewed as a key component of WWC's overall workings. There is much debate in the literature as to whether diversity policies are actually productive and help an organization or whether they are implemented in a way that deflect real change. Our findings, indeed, demonstrate how diversity tropes are often used by racialized organizations to mask the processes that lead to the reproduction and preservation of the existing social order.

As already suggested, diversity literature and more specifically literature addressing multiracial churches demonstrates that diversity can become a way to draw attention away from any meaningful organizational change, ultimately keeping in place policies and practices that reproduce the racial status quo. For example, scholars pose that when racial minorities are integrated into predominantly White spaces, racial diversity does not affect the core culture and practices of the organizations involved (Bell and Hartmann 2007; Berrey 2011; S. Collins 2011; Edwards 2008b); rather, it is treated as an addendum to the overarching organizational structure (Embrick 2011; Marti 2012; Marvasti and McKinney 2011). This can be seen particularly in the absence of Black campus pastors and Black members of the ALT at WWC.

Beyond overly emphasized images of diversity, churches especially in the White evangelical tradition fail at achieving real diversity (Collins 2011; Edwards 2008b; Embrick 2011; Marvasti and McKinney 2011). This makes minorities powerful in the sense that they make significant contributions to the image of diversity, which serves as a competitive advantage for most multiracial churches (Acker 1990; Grazian 2004; Barron 2016). However, these same minorities often find themselves sidelined from positions of power and unable to make significant impact at upper levels. This causes Black members to bear greater burdens in maintaining multiracial congregations (Edwards 2008b; Marti 2012). Thus, existing studies demonstrate that most multiracial churches, including WWC, may in fact use diversity as a smoke screen to hide the ways in which processes of domination and subordination are being reproduced.

In the next section, we will explore the ways in which diversity was framed by interview participants at WWC and how this framing may ultimately reproduce racism and negatively impact the church.

Diversity at Without Walls Church

During the early stages of data collection, it became clear that the interview participants and most of the WWC community valued and uplifted the idea that WWC is racially diverse. Many of the interview participants acknowledged that the diversity of WWC initially drew them and played a factor in their decision to join the community. Chris Fells articulated this as follows: "This is the reason why I joined here. I was drawn here because of the fact when I first pulled up to the church, I saw old, young, Black, White, brown." Mac also described the diversity of the south Florida area and the church as a necessary factor for his family's spiritual development: "It was what drew us to south Florida and ultimately WWC was the fact that, when we're associated with such a big group of White folks in Oklahoma, it's really difficult to explain to our kids how great our God is and how diverse He is, and the fact that the majority of Christians in the free world are not White." Craig also attributed the church's racial makeup as the reason he joined. He commented, "If I'm honest with you, as cliché as it's going to sound because of this interview, it was because of the racial makeup."

The church's racial diversity is also used as a recruitment tool for potential employees and new church leaders. According to Joe, "And many times, it's made us an attractive landing spot for other folks when they see how culturally diverse that we are. I've heard it over and over again from different staff members that come into the organization. They're like, 'Man, one of the reasons I wanted to land here was because this place is so diverse.'" Chris also reinforces the importance of the racial diversity of the WWC staff: "So having a diverse staff, like our staff, I think our staff is very, very diverse, which is why I'm drawn to not just WWC, but the staff here, helps us to reach that."

While interview participants framed diversity in a myriad of ways, including race, age, and class, it was the racial diversity of WWC that initially drew the attention of these individuals. As Bell and Hartmann (2007) found, when Americans describe and discuss diversity, race is at the core of this talk. Although racial diversity of WWC is consistently lifted as a hallmark of the community by members and leaders and was even described as a "picture of heaven," there were several instances in which interview participants expressed their views that perhaps the diversity of WWC did not go far enough. When referencing the ALT, Mac raises the idea that not having a Black member on this team could negatively impact the church's progress: "When they have meetings and we talk about racial diversity or we talk about being a part of what's going on in the Black community right now, it's really difficult for that group to have that conversation without someone present." Grace also suggests that the diversity of the ALT could be improved. "Do I think it could be more diverse? Yeah. I think that I would love to see, in the future, if the Lord would grant us someone of color, I think that that would be special." Prior to this statement, Grace described the ALT as being composed of individuals from Latin and Asian backgrounds, arguably persons who could be considered "people of color." One may infer from her comment that she would like to see a Black person added to this group. Sydney also critiqued the absence of Black leaders atop the church's hierarchy: "I don't understand that personally ... I know our church really wants to be diverse, but if you want it, you got to follow it all the way through ... you cannot feel comfortable saying, well, we have X for Black pastors." These comments reveal that for some, the absence of Blacks at the top tier of leadership is problematic.

Perhaps some of the more salient critiques regarding diversity at WWC stems from the perceived conflation of diversity and equality by community members. In response, Mac comments, "I think our church has taken the posture of we're not racist, we're very diverse. I'm like, just because you're diverse doesn't mean that you're not racist." Tim Smith echoed these sentiments as well. "I think you can be a diverse place but racial equality not be there." He went on to metaphorically reinforce his statement: "And there was an illustration the lady used ... diversity is like being invited to the dance and then racial equality is being asked to dance. So yeah, I believe you can be a diverse place but not have racial equality." As suggested earlier, racialized organizations both reproduce and challenge racialization processes. The criticisms offered by the church members are examples of the thought processes that could challenge the reproduction of racism.

These comments further reveal a contrast in ideology as it relates to the conflation of diversity and racial justice, with diversity being equated with justice or fairness in the organization. As such, our findings reveal that there is a lack of diversity in higher-tier leadership positions and higher rates of diversity in lower-tier leadership positions. The diversity in lower-tier positions allows for the organization to appear more diverse than it is in fact. When Ray's propositions are analyzed within the context of WWC, it is not hard to see how diversity is sidelined and racism is reproduced, as we explore the relationship between racial ideology and resources.

Elements of Racialized Organizations Theory

PROPOSITION ONE: RACIALIZED ORGANIZATIONS SHAPE AGENCY

Ray (2019, 36) defines racialized organizations as "meso-level social structures that limit the personal agency and collective efficacy of subordinate racial groups while magnifying the agency of the dominant racial group." These limitations or constraints include everything from the ability to act, create, learn, and express emotion. Ray argues that one's position in a racialized organizational hierarchy shapes their ability to act. If minorities are at the bottom of a multiracial congregation's hierarchy, it may impact their agency.

According to Ray (2019), agency can be shaped in a few ways, including control over personal time, limiting the range of acceptable emotion, and shaping the organizational vision. An individual's location in a racialized organization can affect how their time is used as well as their ability to shape the future of the organization. How does this relate to WWC? If minorities occupy lower-tier roles within a multiracial congregation, their time may be consumed by more menial activities (e.g., cleaning, parking, etc.) as opposed to shaping policies and values, creating community-focused ministries, and planning for the future of the organization.

Ray also argues that racialized organizations can constrain agency by limiting minorities' range of emotional expressions. As noted earlier, multiracial churches are known to have charismatic worship styles, which include emotional elements. If minorities are encouraged to subdue their emotions in worship or alter the ways in which they react to social injustices, this significantly restricts agency. Ray showed how minorities conforming to racialized organizational scripts can reproduce systems of inequality. What do people of color do in multiracial congregations? Often, minorities are associated with service-oriented tasks. If multiracial congregations overwhelmingly employ minorities as janitors, parking attendants, and so on, this may reproduce systems of inequality, shape the way these tasks are viewed, and lead to the racialization of tasks and positions along with the individuals who occupy those positions and perform those tasks.

The ability of racialized organizations to shape agency can be seen in the ways in which minorities, particularly Blacks, are placed in various staff positions. As previously discussed, a major critique of WWC by those interviewed is the absence of Black campus pastors and Black members of the ALT, the top leadership group. According to Sydney, "We're not doing anything. We have nothing that we're doing that's going to reach that community and that's because we don't have the influence at the top ... even on the ALT ... There is nobody Black on that. Nobody. Ok, so there's that huge problem. That is a problem. Problem, problem, problem. Because you don't even have influence there. You don't have anything. Just a voice. It could be a man, woman, whoever. Just a voice. Someone to say, guys, we need to get out ahead of it." Edwards (2008a, 2008b) found that Black men participate in church activities but are not elevated into upper-tier positions. This finding suggests that the professional agency of Black men is restricted as they are constrained from reaching certain positions. Their time and ability to influence the core of the organization is minimized.

This lack of influence was witnessed firsthand after the death of George Floyd Jr. During this time, not only did the leaders of WWC (teaching pastors) come together for broader discussions concerning the theological framing of injustice for the church, all the secondary leaders in the various campus student ministries also came together for a discussion on racial injustice. What was striking about this conversation is the diversity at the lower levels, which was not seen at the upper levels. Of the nine student ministry leaders who participated, four appeared to be

Black, one White, and the remaining ones were Latinx. This aligns with Barron's (2016) findings, which argue that Black men are overrepresented in second-tier leadership positions of high visibility; however, these same individuals lack the power to move up in leadership at the same rates as their non-Black counterparts, which affects their impact in the organization overall. Significantly, Sydney commented on the number of Black student ministry leaders, "I would say this, I feel that we have Black youth pastors or student pastors because they've been chosen for that purpose to reach urban to reach that demographic. And that bothers me because it's like, okay, well we will put a Black pastor here, here, and here but we don't have one preaching." The overrepresentation of Black student ministry leaders allows WWC to embrace diversity frames while simultaneously marginalizing Blacks from top-tier leadership positions. This is also evidenced by the Mac's previously mentioned account, in which he reflected on the campus leadership of the church's northwest location. He mentioned that the most qualified candidate was Black; however, that candidate would not be considered because of his race. Once again, agency is constrained because of race.

Clearly, a lack of representation in top positions is an issue at WWC. The ALT, top leadership group, has no Black members and there are no Black campus pastors; however, most of the student ministry leadership, the lower tier positions, are made up of Black members. The absence of Black members in top-tier leadership positions suggests that their professional agency may be constrained. Ray (2019) noted that one's position in the hierarchy of an organization is going to impact what one does with their time, how they act, and what they can contribute.

Agency can also be shaped through the regulation of individual's emotional expression. In the aftermath of the death of George Floyd Jr., Craig James described the first communication he received from WWC regarding Floyd's death. This correspondence was a reminder sent to church staff referencing personnel social media policies at WWC. The intent of the correspondence, according to him, was to remind the staff to be aware of their social media comments and postings. Craig mentioned that he took offense to the correspondence because it not only reflected an insensitivity to Floyd's death but also attempted to regulate the responses of the church's employees. Such correspondence was a clear attempt on the church's part to shape and control church personnel's agency, including their emotional responses.

It also appears that agency can be shaped by organizations in ways where it seems as if it those being constrained have a choice. That is to say, the practices and policies of the church can be so impactful as to make it seem that the individuals involved are making personal and individual decisions. For example, Mavelin describes an experience in which she hesitated to affirm a protest in the aftermath of Floyd's death because of her WWC car sticker. This hesitation was borne out of church policies and practices that minimize social activism related to high-profile racial incidences.

> The other day we were driving to school to return some textbooks and she [Mavelin's daughter] saw a group of protestors. And one of the signs said Black Lives Matter, so she wanted to honk, like, "Honk if you're for it," or whatever. However, because of all the bad things that I've seen with the riots and what is their main purpose for this process, is it to hurt people, so I was a little iffy about honking the horn. I go, "Wait, wait, wait. I have a WWC sticker on my car! Hold on, we can't just be joining this protest!"

Although Mavelin expressed hesitancy about supporting the protests because, in her view, they were violent in nature, the presence of WWC signifiers added to her ambivalence. We clearly see agency being shaped by an organization here.

PROPOSITION TWO: LEGITIMATE THE UNEQUAL DISTRIBUTION OF RESOURCES

Closely associated with the first proposition is the second proposition, the legitimation of unequal distribution of resources. This includes the recognition of the role segregation plays in the distribution of resources, which as noted above, goes a long way in propping up traditional racial ideology that implies who deserves what and why (e.g., lack of strong work ethic). According to Ray (2019), racial segregation is a fundamental characteristic of most organizations and is enforced through the distribution of resources. For example, the landmark decision that led to the overturning of the "separate but equal" doctrine came from recognition that resources enjoyed by African Americans were not equal to those of White Americans.

Multiracial "progressive" organizations can also recreate institutional-level segregation. For example, certain hierarchal positions can be associated with racial groups, leading to the overvaluing or devaluing of those positions. As racialized hierarchies become naturalized, feelings of superiority or inferiority can become institutionalized. With respect to WWC, this can include certain staff positions that over time can be associated with dominant group membership while lower level and volunteer positions are made available for members of minority groups. Furthermore, if church membership and leadership is overwhelmingly White, this could legitimate the unequal distribution of resources because there are no minority voices articulating the needs of marginalized community members.

Examples of the unequal distribution of resources came out most clearly around the organizational practice of music inclusion and worship. Researchers have found that music selection is an important factor in the success or failure of multiracial congregations (Ammerman 1997; Becker 1999). This importance is highlighted by many nonwhites who view integration of culturally diverse rituals and worship practices as a sign of their inclusion in the physical space (Dougherty and Huyser 2008). Moreover, music is one of the most important elements of an evangelical service (Chaves 2004; Dougherty and Huyser 2008; Marti 2012), transmitting religious, organizational, and racial identity (Barron 2016). Music is often used as a tool to communicate a White racial organizational identity, which privileges Whiteness and White normative styles of worship (Edwards 2008b; Molotch 1972).

All of this can be seen at WWC. For example, Joe shared, "Once in a while we'll throw a bone and we'll do a song in Spanish or partly in Spanish." Although WWC has the capital, talent, and financial resources to present a variety of different cultural worship styles and music, Joe's comments reveal that these resources are mainly appropriated to suit the worship preferences of Whites. Additionally, Joe, who identifies as White, suggests that the dominant group controls the worship resources and uses culturally diverse worship rituals at "their" discretion. Conversely, Jake, who also identifies as White, critiques the racial homogenization of worship: "Why are we not integrating Gospel music into our worship? We do integrate in Spanish . . . So, that has bothered me. And I think that also too would show an avenue of love to the culture that we're trying to reach." Again, Jake comments on the distribution of worship resources that incorporates Spanish elements, albeit sparingly, but excludes other cultural genres of worship music. By not including various worship styles, the emotional, ritualistic, and cultural expression of many people are constrained, reflecting the racialized character and practices of the WWC organization.

PROPOSITION THREE: RACIALIZATION AND CREDENTIALING

Ray (2019) argued that Whiteness is a credential providing access to resources, legitimizing organizational hierarchies, and expanding the agency of Whites. Although credentials appear to be race neutral, objective, and based on merit, Ray posited that they institutionalize property interests and expand the agency of Whites. For example, studies examining hiring processes found that Whiteness was an important factor in this realm (Bertrand and Mullainathan 2004; Ray 2019; Quillian et al. 2017). Conversely, Ray showed that for Blacks, race becomes a negative credential, reducing their chances of success. For example, despite legal restrictions barring racial discrimination, many employers oppose hiring people of color due to schemas alleging poor work habits and attitudes (Moss and Tilly 2003; Neckerman and Kirschenman 1991; Pager and Karafin 2009; Pager, Western, and Bonikowski 2009). Notably, it was the very recognition of Whiteness as a credential that necessitated affirmative action policies after the civil rights movement, in an effort to change the connection between racial schemas and organizational resources (Ray 2019).

Over the course of the data collection process for this study, Whiteness was never directly referred to as a credential; however, members of the WWC community did reflect on the benefits and privileges of Whiteness, as well as conflating Whiteness and American identity. For example, Grace who identifies racially as White and ethnically as Cuban, described her decision-making process when completing her pre-interview questionnaire: "I chose White I guess because I feel American . . . I'm White, so that's why I chose it. I usually choose White. I guess I feel American because I'm the second generation born in the United States, of my family." As previously covered in chapter 1, the ways in which race and ethnicity impact self-identification is nuanced, particularly for first- and second-generation immigrants, and the ways in which these individuals choose to identify varies. Furthermore, Grace's comments demonstrate the conflation of Whiteness with being American, like Cata's sentiments in the previous chapter.

Thus, in an internationally diverse region of the country, both Whiteness and American citizenship are credentials used by some to differentiate themselves from others in their own racial/ethnic communities. Grace could identify as "Other" on the pre-interview questionnaire, like other interview participants who racially identify as Hispanic; however, she makes the conscious decision to choose White although others do not consider her White. Grace states, "But then my friends that are White American, they're like, 'No, you're pretty Hispanic.' I'm like, 'Really?'" Grace continues to self-identify as White American, despite her identity choice being called into question by others. Perhaps she self-identifies as White because of the credentials that accompany her racial designation.

Closely associated with the idea of Whiteness as a credential is the ideology of White privilege. White privilege can be defined as "the unearthed benefits that flow to Whites in the American racial order—as well as the 'lack of awareness' of this privilege by Whites" (Doane 2003, 7). White privilege emerged as a repeated theme among interview participants, as they acknowledged its existence and the ways in which they benefit from it. For example, Kal shared, "but I am still even living in a culture and a time where, sadly and ultimately, I have a very privileged upbringing, just by being the color that I am." He goes on to say, "I know I'm privileged. I know that I've been given so much, just by my color, but also even in my family's status and all these things. I get it. I understand I'm spoiled out of my mind, I'm privileged beyond belief." Much like racialized credentialing, he admits that his property interests are increased because of his race. The fact that one would recognize and admit their privilege would on the surface seem to be a challenge to racialization processes; however, as previously discussed, when that acknowledgment of White privilege is not used to dismantle White supremacy, it only reproduces racism. This can be seen in Kal's comments regarding his involvement in activities that promote racial equality. He states, "I just haven't had, I guess because of my privilege maybe, I'm just not as incentivized to be as active as I should, with that." Kal admits that although he recognizes his racialized privilege, he does not actively involve himself in causes and efforts that promote racial equality, a value he claims is important. It seems as if Kal does not engage in these activities precisely because of his privilege, which exempts him from experiences of domination, subordination, and racism.

In her interview, Cata, critiqued the notion that White privilege is extended to all Whites. She said, "and somebody having privilege or somebody having whatever . . . Like, there are a lot of poor White people, too, that don't have . . . And if you look at how they're dressed, they're not going to get the job." While Cata advances a very class-based definition of racialized privilege, scholars argue that White privilege is enjoyed by even the poorest of Whites (DuBois 1935). Based on Cata's comments, one could suppose that a class-based understanding of racialized privilege may be used as a tool to defend that very privilege and maintain the racial order by arguing that poor Whites are as marginalized as Blacks and other minorities. Equating the marginalization of poor Whites to that of Blacks and other persons of color ignores their nuanced experiences, rejects the idea of structural inequalities, maintains the racial order, and aids in the reproduction of racism.

PROPOSITION FOUR: RACIALIZED DECOUPLING

According to Ray (2019, 42), "racialized organizations often decouple formal commitments to equity, access, and inclusion from policies and practices that reinforce, or at least do not challenge, existing racial hierarchies." This decoupling allows organizations to maintain a progressive appearance while doing little to overturn racial inequality. Ray argues that diversity and other antidiscrimination policies often serve a public relations role but do little to change the distribution of power within a given organization. Furthermore, there is a lack of enforcement when it comes to policy violations, investigations, and subsequent resolutions. As previously noted, we seek to understand whether there are verbal commitments to social, racial, and economic forms of justice that are not reinforced through the actions of wwc. The findings detailed here indicate that there is indeed racialized decoupling occurring at wwc, specifically in how the values of racial equality are carried out by the organization.

Interview participants were asked about their values as Christians and if the value of racial equality is important to them personally and to the wwc community more broadly. Overwhelmingly, the majority agreed that racial equality is an important value. For example, Kal responded by saying, "It's so important and so ingratiated in the Gospel, of how important it is to treat everyone with equality." Like Cal, Mike simply said, "I think it's very important." Similarly, Sydney responded, "Very important. Paramount. It's really important to me . . . So racial equality is important. It's heavy on my heart." For his part, Craig noted, "Racial equality therefore, I think is assumed in everything. It's tantamount." In the same vein, Vanessa responded, "Yeah, it's very important. It's all around us. You can't ignore it. So this is something that touches everyone that we come in contact with, and it's a part of everything I do." For these individuals, racial equality is rooted in the Gospel and is present in everyone's beliefs and actions. Hojuma also speaks of racial equality as an important component of theology: "Well, as a Christian, our Scripture is clear. There is no difference between races, or ethnic groups, or sexes, or anything. In God's eyes, we are all equal. So as a Christian, that has to be my view, too. That we're all equal." Mac's comments echoed Craig's sentiments: "Is racial equality one of my values as a Christian? I think it's more understood than stated . . . So I would say, yeah, I think it is a value, but it's not stated because it's a value that's always seen."

Some of the individuals interviewed also believed racial equality to be important for WWC generally speaking. According to Grace, "I think as a whole, I think our church is committed to racial equality." Melissa also affirms WWC's commitment to racial equality: "Well, I would say they are very committed to racial equality and bringing in diversity, not just on a Black/White/Hispanic level, on an 'every tribe, tongue, and nation' level." Still, there were some who felt there was room for improvement. Sydney stated:

> I'd like to see more of that on staff. You can't have equality without going the distance. It encompasses a lot. And you can't only have it on your youth teams, and it's just not the same . . . So do I feel they're committed? I feel like they think they are, but they've showed [sic] that they were not really ready for it. And it might be they want input on how to be better. Maybe they want exactly what you're asking, to have more equality. But I still told them the first step in any equality is don't segregate.

For Sydney, WWC does not go far enough in the pursuit of racial equality, specifically in terms of better representation of certain groups within higher levels of church leadership. Racial equality among the staff also serves as a point of contention for Tim Smith. He says, "Do I think racial equality is a value of WWC? Yes and no. From the Christian side, I would say yes. From an organizational side of maybe sometimes in hiring and different things, maybe not. It's not thought of as much." Like Sydney, Tim calls on WWC to go the distance and not just uplift racial equality from a theological or biblical standpoint but also make it a factor in hiring decisions, particularly for top-tier leadership positions.

While WWC is critiqued by some for not going far enough in its approach to racial equality, particularly in regard to hires, racialized decoupling at WWC can be seen in other ways as well. One of these is the highlighting of diversity as opposed to teaching and talking about racial equality. In Hans' view, "But as we are trying to build the church that God has called us to build, we celebrate the diversity that God has brought us, as we acknowledge it, but I don't know that we directly teach on it." As noted earlier by Tim, there is a difference between diversity and racial equality. Hans acknowledges that diversity is celebrated while conversations around racial equality are minimized, allowing for WWC to seem progressive while doing nothing to change or challenge the racial order. Hans goes on to give an example:

> For me, let's say I'm teaching a topic. I'm trying to think of something that would be a good example. Let's say I was teaching through the book of Exodus, and we learned about Moses marrying an Ethiopian woman. Well, that means she's probably Black. So, because of the world that we live in today, I would most likely make a point of that, again to celebrate it. But I guess I couldn't say that I intentionally try to think about okay, how can I reinforce the value of racial equality in staff meeting today, or how can I try to do it. If and when things come up, I try to address it, but I guess one of the biggest things, I give time and space to the things that I feel like we need to develop in, that we need to grow in.

Like other interviewees, Hans highlights diversity, especially in theological and biblical contexts; however, it does not translate administratively into ways that allow for racial equality to take place tangibly and materially. This is the racialized decoupling Ray (2019) argues is a hallmark of racialized organizations. On the surface there seems to be a commitment to an ostensible notion of racial equality, which is really diversity, and no commitment to formalized practices that reinforce true racial equality. Joe also makes a similar observation: "The church's commitment to it (racial equality) is good. Does the church proactively seek out conversations to engage in some of the national issues regarding it? No, they don't." He goes on to say, "Our commitment, it's somewhat strong. Here's why I say that. It's not something that we actively preach against and it's not something that we actively talk about on a whole lot of . . . Like within the organization very strong. Outside of the organization, it's not something that we advocate for or go out of our way to talk about. I don't think that's a critique, I think that's just the reality." Thus, although Joe states that the church's commitment to racial equality is strong, he highlights that the church does not proactively engage in conversations, sermons, or advocacy for racial justice and against racial injustice. Yet, if these things are not happening, it casts serious doubt on the strength of wwc's commitment to racial equality. Here is another example of the stark difference between what is being said in interviews and the public celebration of diversity and the tangible and material ways in which the commitment to racial justice is actually being acted out (or not, in this case).

In another example of racialized decoupling, when asked about how important racial equality is to his Christian values, Mike responded:

> I think it's very important. It's just as important as any injustice or anything that we would say is wrong. There's no room in the Christian faith and the teachings of Jesus to hate a person because of their race. We see examples of people hating in the Bible. And we see examples of people that are living out what God, and what Jesus taught, and what the Bible taught . . . I think that it's very important. I don't think it's any more important or any less important than any other injustice that the Bible would talk about. If it is wrong, then we as Christians are to speak out against it just as our name would imply. Being Christ like. He would speak out against an injustice. Then we would, too. Then it would be important.

From Mike's comments, one could assume that racial justice is paramount when it comes to his Christian values and what he believes the values of his faith community should be. He intimates that Christians should be fearless when it comes to calling out racism and other forms of discrimination and justice. To do this is to follow in the footsteps of Jesus. Yet, in the next breath he seems to take a contradictory position. When it comes to affirming Black lives, Mike states, "I would prefer and I think the safest course of action is to stay away from anything even remotely political so that we can retain integrity and be able to teach the Bible and what it teaches, and nothing else." The fight for justice can often be construed as political. Whether one considers the 2016 election, the Unite the Right rally in Charlottesville, Virginia, NFL protests, or the death of George Floyd, all of these events are both racialized and politicized in nature. Although Mike believes in speaking out against injustice, his subsequent comments offer little to no room for this to happen in practice.

Sources of Change in Racialized Organizations

To reiterate, Ray (2019) defined organizations as racial structures and the primary place in which racial meanings and resources are contested. The challenge to racialization processes that occur in organizations can be the result of both external and internal factors. Externally, Ray (2019) argued that three factors can alter the racialization of organizations: social movements, changes in macro-level policies (e.g., immigration), and the degree and relative level of organizational reliance on the state. Internal sources of organizational change can occur due to an attempt to garner greater market share, diversity programs, and conscious attempts to alter the distribution of resources. While there is evidence that both external and internal sources of change are occurring at wwc, as it relates to the research objectives of this book, we pay particular attention to social movements as a source of external change for wwc as a racialized organization.

External Sources of Organizational Racialization

Of the types of external sources of organizational racialization, the impacts of social movements seemed to be most salient in the wwc community, especially after the death of George Floyd Jr. in May 2020. Ray (2019, 43) described social movements as the "clearest attempts to alter racialized organizations," in that they can form into organizations and associations that channel material and social resources in ways that oppose dominant racialization processes, potentially altering racial structures.

The organization of these social movements can be seen in the BLM movement and the demonstrations that erupted in the United States and beyond even prior to the murder of George Floyd Jr. Since 2014 this social movement has given rise to protests in response to the deaths of Michael Brown, Tamir Rice, Freddie Gray, Philando Castile, Alton Sterling, and Walter Scott. BLM also joined in with counterprotesters at the 2017 Unite the Right rally in Charlottesville and was supported by various athletes who kneeled at sporting events across the country to draw attention to racial injustice. As mentioned in the introduction of this book, the demonstrations that took place after Floyd's murder were not only numerous but also received the attention of corporate America, which channeled millions of dollars in resources to Black organizations and causes. In terms of our case study, these social movements also impacted the racialization of wwc, which addressed the topic of racial injustice in newfound ways, much more so than it had done prior to Floyd's murder and the subsequent social movement explosion.

When we interviewed Darian, he elaborated on why these social movements caused wwc to deviate from its normal response to these kinds of events:

> Yeah. Yeah. Let's be real. The media attention and shame on the church. And even us as wwc, shame on us that it had to be this much protesting, and rioting, and media attention for us to say, "Okay, we've got to address this." And again,

not that we've never touched race, but we've always touched it very sort of lightly, not pointedly, not directly on the topic of race. We are a systematic Bible teaching church, in other words, we just go through books of the Bible, and wherever it lands, if it lands on that subject then, yes, we will heavily address it. But I want to say that in the past, maybe five years, it's come up maybe once a year in the text that we're reading.

Darian admits that prior to the Floyd murder, wwc rarely discussed the topic of race and when discussed, it was touched on "lightly"; however, he insists that the social movements and media attention following Floyd's murder caused the church to change directions and address this topic in unprecedented ways. Grace, in turn, corroborated Darian's interpretation of events. She comments, "But I don't think there's been an entire sermon on race and racism, until recently... So I'm thankful that, maybe we didn't do such a good job in the past, but we addressed it this time, which I think was really helpful."

Jakes offered observations based on a more expansive timeline that also reveals silence on the part of the church when it comes to matters regarding race: "In twenty-five years, I've never seen a racial upheaval or anything happen until this time with George Floyd, which could be a good thing because maybe it was just swept under the rug." There seems to be unanimous agreement that Floyd's murder and the social movements thereafter served as an inflection point for wwc.

This inflection point not only caused wwc to engage in conversations about race and racism, it also caused members of the community to become active in social movements. Gina, an African American woman, shared:

> I haven't been to a BLM march, just because I've never been to one of those events before. But as soon as that opportunity came on Sunday, and I was free, me and my husband and more members of the church, we went to the interfaith prayer walk, and peaceful protest. Because at the same time, I want to show that I do understand, and I'm aware and I see, and as I'm learning, I'm taking those steps as much as I can just to show support and express the same emotions that a lot of people feel as well that are impacting the African American communities.

Gina's comments reveal that she was previously unaffiliated with BLM as a social movement. After the death of Floyd, this changed. She, along with other members of wwc, became involved with BLM in an attempt to align herself with others who are shining a light on the challenges African Americans face. She went on to say, "We know that showing up and doing one prayer walk and one peaceful protest, just like the guy said, there, that doesn't fix it all. But it's continuously taking those steps and putting forth that effort, that you show that there is a presence, that this will be something that will continually be done . . . I've never been a peaceful protest before." For Gina, BLM as a social movement caused her to do something she had never done before, engage in a social protest. Not only did she engage in this protest, other members of the WWC community also participated. Thus, for us it is clear that the emergence of BLM and WWC members' participation in this social movement fits Ray's model (2019) of outside forces challenging the racialization processes internal to an organization.

When we interviewed Grace, her comments notably revealed that church leaders are also a part of the social movements taking place in south Florida in the wake of the Floyd murder: "We have pastors in our church that are out protesting . . . We have some of our pastors that are out doing prayer walks and are part of the peaceful protests here, which is a beautiful thing." Grace also describes how the external social movements are impacting WWC internally: "Then we have some that don't feel comfortable going to the protests but are obviously still burdened and hurt about what's happened." She goes on to say that this morphed into a desire to find resources and conversation guides to help children's ministry leaders and parents talk to children about racial injustices. Although the curriculum used by the children's ministry now has resources in this area, this was not yet true the week after Floyd's murder. In response to the absence of resources, Grace says, "So, we decided that, 'Okay, we can't find anything, so we're going to make up our own. We're going to make our own parent resource of how parents can talk to their kids about race and racism.' So, we pivoted and we did that. I know our student ministry did something similar, and they had a discussion for their Friday night service." Grace's comments are another example of how social movements may be sources of external change for racialized organizations. The social movements sparked by the Floyd murder caused the children's ministry to "pivot" to have unprecedented conversations and provide resources about race and racism. Material and social resources were channeled in a way that challenged organizational racialization processes.

Mac also describes the process of how Floyd's murder and the subsequent social movements served as a source of change for WWC:

> Yeah, so I can tell you this. We've had to regroup and we took a very passive approach in the beginning. So I think a lot of our communication has come from not saying enough. So I was proud of our leadership team that they came out and acknowledged that . . . So our church was extremely passive in the beginning and, over the weekend . . . Basically, George Floyd's death, we had sent out maybe a tweet or text or things like that. Didn't say anything about it that weekend. Then that following week we had a meeting where our Black female and male staff

members really got a chance to speak up and have their voice heard here at the church about how we responded. So we completely changed directions after that. So that's what the policies had to do with is allowing people to speak up, allowing people to join in safe protests and things like that.

Mac acknowledges that WWC's initial response was very passive, perhaps reflecting the church's traditional response to events of this nature. Mac also describes how WWC changed course due to the media attention and the sheer size of the social movements that ensued. He goes on to give more details about what it has looked like for WWC to change direction in the wake of Floyd's murder:

So we had . . . Let's see, church-wide communication stating our stance against racial injustice. We have had round table discussions with our senior leadership as well as on down the line. So, we had round table discussions with Black people, Hispanic people, White people, things like that to be educated and informed. We have come up with policies as far as how to actively be a part of what God's doing in the movement since George Floyd's death. So yeah, I think there's been a ton of stuff that we have acknowledged and woke up I guess and started to engage in those conversations.

Here, Mac describes how external sources of organizational racialization challenged preexisting approaches to injustices, gave voice to the stories of the marginalized, created new policies, and encouraged civic engagement, which will hopefully lead to a more just organizational praxis in the future.

Interviewees also mentioned that they hope WWC stays committed to social justice going forward. For example, Darian said, "We had to do something about it. And now we realize it, we have to say something. And we just can't give it that one night or that one talk." Allyssa described what she sees as ongoing efforts to ensure that these changes remain at WWC: "I think we have stuff lined up even in July, like things that we're continuously going to be discussing and putting a strategy in place of how we can make progress." Other interviewees commented about how they appreciated the direction WWC was going in as it relates to conversations and social activism. Recalling her participation in the prayer walk and peaceful protest, Gina shared:

Those that were out there, I was like, these are the like little steps that they're trying to take. They're making us aware, they're showing us that they're going to be there, and we can join and show up too . . . So I feel like if what I've seen just by those steps and those efforts, is something that will continue, I feel it will be good.

Here, Gina refers to church leaders who joined in the peaceful protests. For her, their presence also affirmed her ongoing participation in these kinds of causes.

Whether or not the social movements that occurred in the summer of 2020 will serve as a catalyst for permanent change at WWC remains to be seen; however, Floyd's murder and the global response it garnered tremendously impacted and changed the ways in which WWC responds to racial injustice at least in the short term. This change led to new conversations, engaging the voices of the unheard, and creating policies that allow for greater involvement in the pursuit of social justice. All of this challenges racialization processes and how material and social resources are channeled and allocated within the organization.

Conclusion

Countering the notion of organizations as race neutral, Ray's theoretical framework argues that organizations are racial structures that reproduce (and challenge) racialization processes. He (2019) describes four pillars that are essential to this racialization process and understanding how racial ideology and inequality are reproduced in organizations: (1) the shaping of agency; (2) the legitimation of the unequal distribution of resources; (3) linking race and credentialing; and (4) racialized decoupling, all of which are evident at WWC. Based on Ray's groundbreaking theoretical work, WWC fits the criteria of a racialized organization and findings in this chapter demonstrate that racialization processes are indeed occurring within the organization, with both reproducing and challenging the racial order.

Specifically, we found that while WWC is understood as a diverse and even progressive organization, this diversity does not seem to impact its core practices and culture, in line with research findings from other scholars (Edwards 2008a, 2008b). Furthermore, diversity at WWC is touted as positive and progressive; however, when top-tier leadership positions are examined along with worship, diversity itself seems to be lacking, which greatly impacts the workings of the church. At the same time, as articulated by several interviewees, the church seems to make a false equivalency between diversity and equality, a notion challenged by some of its members. Positions of influence seem to be restricted to certain groups, resulting in subordination of Black folks and the limitation of what they bring to the church. This is particularly noteworthy in the music that is played during services.

Turning now more specifically to Ray's theory, the professional agency of Blacks is restricted at WWC in that none serve on the ALT or as campus pastors and worship resources are unevenly distributed to suit the interests and styles of

Whites. Additionally, Whiteness as a credential may be seen in how some members choose to identify as well as their acknowledging of privilege that flows from Whiteness. Lastly, racialized decoupling occurs in that there is a verbal commitment to racial equality without intentional pursuit of this equality through conversation, sermons, engagement, and action.

At the same time, we found external challenges to these processes. This can primarily be seen in the impact the murder of George Floyd Jr. and the social movements thereafter had on wwc. In response to these events, wwc for the first time engaged in conversations, developed resources, acknowledged racial injustices, and participated in social activism efforts. These actions directly challenged racialization processes as members of the wwc community began to scrutinize their policies and decisions in hopes of creating a more just society and organizational praxis.

CHAPTER 5

Where Does All of This Fit?

Returning to Where We Began

In this book, we have sought to understand issues facing a south Florida multiracial church related to race and social activism. More specifically, we asked whether leaders and members of WWC actively reproduce racism and hurt social activism efforts. If so, what are the ways in which they do this? We were particularly interested in this question considering the heightened attention among scholars to White evangelical Christians, particularly their participation in the 2016 U.S. presidential election in support of Donald Trump and their role in the reproduction of the dominant racial ideology (Mehta et al. 2022).

Since the 2016 election, there has been insufficient attention to the role of multiracial churches and the ways in which they may reproduce racism in an extraordinary period in U.S. history, which includes the death of George Floyd Jr. and the rise of Black Lives Matter. With this goal in mind, we sought to extend the work of several prominent scholars in the social sciences, including Eduardo Bonilla-Silva (2018) on color-blind frames, Assata Zerai (2011) on multiracial churches, colorblindness, and social activism, and Victor Ray (2019) on racialized organizations theory. As noted in an earlier chapter, our intent was not to call out or label any one member or leader of the church as racist. Rather, we sought to understand the underlying ideology, policies, and practices that may reproduce racism and inequality even in a multiracial church without, as poignantly stated by Bonilla-Silva (2018), a racist in sight.

Using these works as a foundation, we asked three main questions. First, we wanted to assess whether the WWC used color-blind frames to contextualize and ultimately dismiss racialized events and social activism in this "most racial" period of U.S. history. Eduardo Bonilla-Silva (2018) posed that color-blind racism is the dominant ideology in the United States today (although some argue this is changing with the rise of Donald Trump and MAGA). Color-blind frames are prevalent in all facets of life, ranging from humor to the classroom. Accordingly, the question at hand was whether this malleable yet pernicious ideology leaks into multiracial contexts like the WWC, where members come from different racial and ethnic backgrounds. Some argue that multiracial churches can overcome racial division by creating deeper relationships among congregants and by giving White congregants insights into the problems and hardships facing Black folks and other people of color. However, more recent scholarship has raised questions about this promise and raised doubts about the liberalizing effect of such multiracial churches, especially when it comes to the topic of race and racism, by arguing that such churches are not immune to dominant racial order and ideology found in the United States today (Edwards 2008a, 2008b).

Second, extending the work of Zerai (2011), we sought to assess more specifically if and what color-blind frames associated with the church's theological teachings are used to oppose racism and/or social activism. Along with Zerai, others have questioned how religious teachings are used to handle critical issues of race (Oyakawa 20019). And third, we sought to move past ideology and assess whether the reproduction of racism can be found in the inner workings of WWC. Using the work of Ray (2019) on racialized organizations, we sought to uncover whether policies and practices used by this multiracial church work to reproduce racism rather than to prop up and celebrate racial differences.

In this final chapter, we review key findings and explain what they mean for WWC as well as for race relations in the United States more generally. We then explore the broader implications of these findings for race and racism scholarship.

Key Findings

As described in chapter 1, previous research has found that on average, multiracial churches fail to address racial inequalities within the congregational setting and that when those inequalities are addressed, church leadership often sides with the interests of Whites (Edwards 2008a, 2008b). For example, worship preferences of Whites are deferred to more than the worship preferences of other racial groups in these churches. Furthermore, multiracial congregations fail to acknowledge systemic racial inequalities and are unlikely to support civic and political efforts that seek to redress these (Zerai 2011). This creates a situation where many multiracial congregations value visual representations of diversity while simultaneously marginalizing the voices and experiences of racial minorities and preventing them from accessing key leadership positions, all while maintaining White socioreligious norms.

We found WWC to be in line with preexisting scholarship on multiracial congregations through racial narratives used by leaders and members that relied on the dominant racial ideology and church teachings. While both leaders and members are important for understanding the culture of the church and how they deal with issues of race, it is leaders who have the ability to manipulate the workings of the church, including the messages sent to worshipers and the policies and practices implemented. We found WWC to be similar to site 2 in Zerai (2011) in several fundamental ways: WWC did not have a focus on social change, particularly before the murder of George Floyd Jr.; the church sparingly acknowledged racism; it maintained homogenous leadership; and it provided little space for Whites to understand the experiences and views of Black congregants.

In chapter 2, we examined the ways WWC used the frames and style of colorblindness as described by Bonilla-Silva (2018) to produce and reproduce the dominant racial ideology. While this is not groundbreaking, we did want to assess whether the dominant frames of our time did in fact predominate in the data. In a way, we felt this was a baseline measure of how this organization dealt with race and racial issues. Accordingly, we found that Whites, Blacks, and individuals of other races, many of whom are church leaders, trafficked in colorblindness. This is in line with the scholarship of Bonilla-Silva (2018) in that the reproduction of this ideology is not dependent on sole usage by Whites. Other racial groups also incorporated the frames and style of colorblindness into their own racial ideology.

As developed by Bonilla-Silva, the frames of color-blind ideology include abstract liberalism, naturalism, cultural racism, and minimization of race. Although there is reason to believe sufficient interracial contact could foster more progressive attitudes among members and leaders at WWC, the pervasive use of the naturalization and cultural racism frames demonstrates that the color-blind ideology is quite malleable and alive even within a multiracial religious context. The data demonstrate that the stereotypes of racial groups are upheld even as members worship, work, and communicate with individuals of differing racial and ethnic backgrounds. In addition to the repeated use of the frames of color-blind ideology, we found the style of colorblindness employed when church members talked about race. Those interviewed tended to avoid the use of direct racial language and engaged in projections and rhetorical incoherence when discussing racial topics. Such styles allowed for very diluted discussion of real racial issues.

In chapter 3, we extended the work of Assata Zerai (2011), which examined three multiracial congregations. Zerai posed that when the social justice counterframe is minimized, multiracial congregations practice colorblindness and uphold the racial status quo. Conversely, she noted that multiracial congregations that embraced social justice as a counterframe actively combated colorblindness and other forms of domination. To this end, we found in the data three examples of what we termed socio-theological color-blind frames used by WWC to minimize the social justice counterframe. We identified these frames as theologizing racism as sin, theologizing justice, and politicizing racism and justice. When used, the intended effect is to negate the need to pursue social and racial justice through action. These frames seek to define racism in theological terms such as "sin," portray social justice attempts as futile considering an all-powerful deity, Jesus Christ, who upon His return will restore justice, and politicize racism and justice in a way that asks the members and leaders to remain silent and not offend any individual's political sensibilities. The ultimate outcome of these socio-theological frames is to deem any humanistic social justice efforts on part of the church as political, divisive, and ineffective. Most interesting, it seems the concept diversity as a positive value was used to suppress action because the church did not want to alienate its White members.

Chapter 4 moved the discussion away from racial ideology to assess the policy and practices of the church and how they may contribute to the problems of race in this multiracial context. In his work on racialized organizations theory, Ray (2019) argued that organizations are not race neutral; rather, they can be racial structures that both reproduce and challenge racialization processes. One way that such processes reproduce racism is through constraining the agency of Black folks and other people of color in the organization. Indeed, we found this to be the case at WWC, where the agency of Blacks was constrained by the lack of leadership positions at the top of the organization, including within the ALT as well as among campus pastors. Such an observation is noteworthy given that Black members were overrepresented in lower-tier leadership positions, particularly within the student ministry. Furthermore, agency was also shaped by WWC's initial response to the murder of George Floyd Jr., in which the leadership reminded employees to be aware of their social media postings that could hurt the church and its members.

Ray (2019) also noted that racism is reproduced when resources are unequally distributed. At WWC, it was clear that this was the case. For example, the practice of music selection was restricted, communicating that the organization deferred to White identity in that there were rarely moments in which music was performed in Spanish and there was no Gospel music performed at all. Moreover, worship resources were clearly being used to suit the preferences of White members. Another finding, one highlighted by Ray (2019) as key to reproduction of racism, included the observation that members of the church view Whiteness as a positive credential, as Latinx individuals repeatedly chose to self-identify as White although others perceived them as nonwhite. There was also a conflation of Whiteness and American identity and citizenship. Finally, in line with Ray's (2019) idea of decoupling, we found that there was a fundamental gap between vocalized commitments to racial equality and actual tangible behaviors that lead to that equality. This led us into an exploration of how Floyd's murder served as an external source of change, leading WWC to have conversations and engage in social protests in the name of racial equality.

Broader Implications and Impact

What do these findings mean overall and for WWC in particular? First, they confirm that an ideology described as racist can be produced and reproduced in a multiracial religious context. Indeed, at WWC, the color-blind frames and styles developed by Eduardo Bonilla-Silva (2018) saturated the data, indicating that members of WWC, a south Florida multiracial congregation, use these elements of colorblindness in many of the ways Bonilla-Silva found over two decades ago among individuals in the general population. The major difference is that while the original color-blind frames found by Bonilla-Silva were there, this sample spoke from more of a socio-religious context.

Significantly, these elements were found in a multiracial congregation and not a predominantly White congregation. For WWC, this means such a context does not shield members and leaders from deleterious ideologically driven frames, which places Black folks and other persons of color in subordinated positions and minimizes the issues they face with racism and discrimination in the past and today. Accordingly, this research demonstrates that Whites and White organizations do not have to be the sole propagators or even the majority in a space for this ideology to breathe. Indeed, racism can exist without racists (Bonilla-Silva 2018). While White members utilized these elements of colorblindness in the church, so did Black, Asian, and Latinx members. As such, Black folks and other people of color are not only routinely affected by color-blind racism through oppression but they are also, in some instances, complicit in its reproduction.

In this case, the broader issue is that the WWC, despite being multiracial, acts as a conduit for the production and reproduction of a pernicious racial ideology that places the blame for inequality at the feet of marginalized groups themselves. Thus, rather than be a place of worship that seeks to promote the teachings of Christ and disrupt the harsh realities of racial division and discrimination that plague U.S. society as a whole, WWC allows for and even joins in its perpetuation.

Second, our research is significant because it revealed additional color-blind frames, which we termed "socio-theological," born out of a color-blind theology used to defend the racial order and minimize social justice. The ways in which this color-blind theology appeared in the data were significant, especially to the field of sociology of religion in general and to WWC in particular. We extended the work of Zerai (2011) by identifying several socio-theological frames, including theologizing sin and racism, theologizing justice, and politicizing racism and justice. Each of these frames minimizes discussion of racism and social activism by leaning into theological teachings, ultimately maintaining the racial status quo. These frames allow for a more nuanced understanding of how theology can act as a suppressant of progress and justice, which should provide insights to race and religion scholars as well as members and leaders in these multiracial churches. Again, like the color-blind frames of Bonilla-Silva, such framing efforts prevent action and minimize critical discussion, ultimately upholding a perspective inimical to the emancipation of marginalized groups.

Third, our research extends Victor Ray's racialized organizations theory, initially publicized in 2019. Since that time, Ian Carrillo (2021) utilized Ray's theory along with color-blind ideology to understand the racial processes of sugar-ethanol mills in Brazil. Similarly, we used Ray's framework to show how, in the case of the WWC, racialized schemas intersect with organizational resources to reproduce racism. We discovered that WWC constrains the agency of Blacks through professional limitations, distributes worship resources unequally, makes verbal commitments to racial equality without action, and uses Whiteness as a credential. Notably, these findings demonstrate how diversity itself is used to distract from the racialized inequities occurring within the congregation.

Further, and also relevant to Ray's theory, our research demonstrates how major racial upheavals can act as external sources of change for racialized organizations, potentially altering racial structures and how resources are distributed. For example, the social movements in the aftermath of George Floyd's death significantly changed the ways in which WWC responded to racial injustice and participated in socially conscious advocacy. This is significant for organizational theory in that it gives credence to the notion that the racial dimension of such social movements can drastically change the policies, programs, and character of organizations.

Thus, our research not only zeroed in on the ideology and processes that lead to the reproduction of racism but also included possible challenges to this process.

Colorblindness, the dominant racial ideology in the United States, lays the foundation both for its own reproduction and challenges to it. These challenges may not always be reflected in research because the focus is often the mechanisms that lead to the reproduction of this ideology; however, this research captured data that showed some challenges to these processes. For example, in chapter 3, Mike critiques wwc's decision to minimize the social justice counterframe and not be socially active. Sydney also challenges wwc's color-blind approach that mandates racism should not be preached about on Sunday morning. Moreover, in chapter 4, Mac and Tim Smith both vehemently critique the conflation of diversity and racial equality, challenging the idea that just because an organization is diverse, it also experiences racial equality. Lastly, in the same chapter, several members of wwc described how Floyd's murder inspired them to become more socially conscious and active. All these examples show church members challenging the dominant racial ideology.

Fourth, our research expands the scope and conversation regarding color-blind ideology. Most research on the topic focuses on the White/Black binary (Mehta et al. 2022; Manning, Hartman, and Gerteis 2015; Todd, Spanierman, and Aber 2010; Tynes and Markoe 2010; Barr and Neville 2008). Some of this work has also been on multiracial congregations and is described in earlier chapters; however, our study incorporates Asian Americans and to a large degree, Latinxs. Furthermore, the implications of identity were included to provide more nuance to our understanding of how the dominant racial ideology was reproduced. For example, we discussed how this affects non–African American Blacks and White Hispanics within the congregation: the way these groups think about race and their own racial identification can provide more opportunities for the exploration of colorblindness. American racial ideology is not just Black or White; for wwc, this means that even marginalized group members can borrow from dominant narratives that minimize issues facing Black folks and other persons of color, meaning that everyone is acculturated and can consume these ideas, regardless of race.

Conclusion

In the end, we hope our research informs multiracial churches and church leaders across the country. The ways in which we "do" and talk about race in these settings are powerful and can validate or invalidate the lived experiences of marginalized groups, ultimately those the church is hoping to serve. In today's environment, race is more salient a topic than ever before. To think the church can skirt these issues to placate certain church members is surely misguided and may lead to broader fissures and ruptures in the end. Equally as powerful as race, religion is a major force in this country. Although society is becoming more secularized, the historical role religion has played in this country is undeniable and continues to play out in significant ways. Congregants look to pastors and other church leaders to shed light on what the Bible teaches when it comes to race, racism, and social justice. The intentional avoidance of these topics robs all those involved of the opportunity to engage in dialogue, learn, and grow spiritually, religiously, and socially. Furthermore, for some, the avoidance of these conversations on race legitimizes the reproduction of racism as a naturally occurring phenomena and allows for colorblindness to proliferate.

Perhaps most devastating of all is the idea that certain lives are not publicly being affirmed by these congregations. For many, faith is a life-giving and life-affirming force. To be silent as Blacks are being murdered in the streets may suggest to the most vulnerable that their lives, experiences, emotions, and so on, are not important or should not be affirmed. Multiracial congregations can be transformative for their communities and society. These congregations, including WWC, have the opportunity to create a model for multiracial dialogue, justice, and the eradication of structural inequalities. It is our hope that this research can be a catalyst for change.

To this end, we hope this book provides readers with insights into how racism is reproduced even in a multiracial context created to transcend racial differences. It is often easier to envision a White church producing such deleterious views and outcomes, because race and racism are issues Whites do not typically have to consider for themselves and their children. However, what about contexts where most congregants are Black folks and other people of color, who do have experiences with racism and discrimination? This book speaks to this question and more, showing that these churches struggle with some of the same issues facing White churches. At times, the WWC did not handle these issues well at all.

These findings are not meant to problematize WWC and similar churches but to show how pervasive racial ideology is even in places we think should be more empathetic, understanding, and insightful. However, we want to make clear that our findings reveal less about the individual members and leaders and more about the structural processes that prop up a racial social system that benefits one group often at the expense of other, more marginalized groups. Although we highlighted and referenced individual comments, we hope to have shown how these individual thoughts are symptomatic of organizational culture and the dominant racial ideology. These findings are also meant to expose policies and practices implemented in these same spaces, not just WWC, and demonstrate how these contribute to racial inequality. Of course, ideology, policies, and practices are not mutually exclusive. Ideology is the force that rationalizes and even supports policies and practices that maintain racial inequality in an organization particularly and in society more generally. In a sense, they are greatly linked to each other, working together to produce racial outcomes that maintain an unequal system.

The heightened national attention to racial inequalities, coupled with the videoed chronicling of Floyd's murder, caused millions to pour into the streets demanding justice for Floyd in the summer of 2020. The impact of both the COVID-19 pandemic and the murder of George Floyd Jr. may be seen in the progress WWC has made when it comes to their policies, dialogues, sermons, and overall commitment to racial justice. Our data revealed evidence that such forces can lead to change. Accordingly, it will be interesting to see if this progress continues at WWC into the future, leading to a more racially progressive multiracial organization where counterframes are created to combat the dominant racial ideology. Alternatively, will progress falter, resulting in an organization that continues to prop up the current racial order? As sociologists who aspire to effect positive societal change, it is our hope that multiracial church leaders across the country will read this book and examine their churches' ideologies, policies, and practices in an effort to combat colorblindness in their own specific contexts. This work is challenging, can be divisive, and has implications administratively, socially, and theologically; however, for those churches serious about addressing the needs and speaking to the lived experiences of *all* their members, this work is necessary. Additionally, it is our hope that it won't take another George Floyd Jr. for multiracial churches to begin a self-examination. Although the global demonstrations and unity were powerful, we must remember they came at the expense of a lost life and the imprisonment of others. The dismantling of the racial and social order should not claim any more lives than it already has. Let us collectively work together to atone for our original sin. In the words of the Reverend Dr. Martin Luther King Jr. on that fateful day in 1963, "No, no, we are not satisfied, and we will not be satisfied until justice rolls down like waters and righteousness like a mighty stream" (King 1963).

APPENDIX

Sample

For this study, we sought to interview a cross section of the church, including campus pastors, members of the ALT, staff, and volunteers. We ultimately interviewed twenty-one members from WWC, twelve males and nine females. Everyone in the sample was over the age of eighteen and consistently attended WWC for at least three months. They ranged in age from twenty-five to eighty-five years old, with an average age of forty. This is in line with demographic data provided by WWC, which shows the average adult age of members to be forty-one. While the church collects demographic data, it does not collect information on race or ethnicity. The average duration of church attendance for the members in the sample was five-plus years. This is important because it reveals that the vast majority of interviewees have been familiar with WWC for quite some time. The racial and ethnic groups represented are as follows: Whites (n=13), Blacks (n=4), Asian (n=1), Native Hawaiian and Pacific Islander = 1, other (n=2). The two individuals who selected "other" identified as Afro-Latino/Native American and Hispanic, respectively. It is also essential to recognize that of the thirteen individuals who identified as White, eight also identified as Hispanic.

Professionally, this sample represents a cross-section of the various levels of employment within WWC. We interviewed a member of the ALT (n=1), campus pastors (n=5), ministry directors (n=6), and lower-level ministry staff and volunteers (n=9).

Methodology

In order to explore the reproduction of racism (through ideology—ways of interpreting society that benefit those in power [Bonilla-Silva 2018]—and practices) on the part of WWC, we implemented a three-part study including participant observation, content analysis, and in-depth interviews. Data collection occurred from June 2019 to October 2020.

PARTICIPANT OBSERVATION

Scholars such as Bernard (1994) and Schensul, Schensul, and LeCompte (1999) outline the importance of participant observation as a research tool that allows the researcher to identify and guide relationships with informants; helps the researcher get the feel for how things are organized and prioritized, how people interrelate, and what the cultural parameters are; shows the researchers what the cultural members deem important in manners, leadership, politics, social interaction, and taboos; helps the researcher become known to cultural members, thereby facilitating the research process; and provides the researcher with a source of questions to be addressed with participants. Due to the coronavirus pandemic, we were limited to only four site visits, resulting in about twelve hours of observations. The initial visit occurred the summer of 2019. We went back to visit the church during one of the regularly scheduled worship services as well as to assist in the setup. We also had the opportunity to visit the main campus of WWC in January of 2020 for a special all-staff meeting. This gathering opened with worship followed by a "vision" message from the lead pastor. Following the message, the group of about one hundred staff dispersed for their various staff meetings. We attended the meeting with the campus pastors as well as the southwest location campus staff meeting. We were also able to have casual conversations with several staff members who served at other locations. In total, during these periods of observation, we took notes that we were able to revisit during the analysis phase of the research project.

CONTENT ANALYSIS

We conducted a content analysis of the church's website and social media, including Twitter, YouTube, Facebook, and Instagram. Data consisted of social media posts dating back to 2016, with attention placed on posts related to the 2016 U.S. presidential election, the August 12, 2017, Unite the Right rally in Charlottesville, the NFL protests led by Colin Kaepernick, and the May 25, 2020, death of George Floyd Jr. in Minneapolis. These events were chosen because of the overt role of race and racism in their unfolding as well as the amount of media attention they garnered. These racialized events were also included in the interview questionnaire detailed later in this appendix. Relating to these events, the content analysis sample included six video postings and three picture posts. It is important to note that the sample that constituted the content analysis came from postings that appeared on all social media platforms. While the content is the same, the comments section of each post across all platforms was examined to determine if members of the community reproduced racial ideology in their responses.

Interviews

We conducted nineteen qualitative interviews with twenty-one staff members and volunteers of WWC. Two of the interviews were joint interviews with married couples. We employed a snowball sampling method in order to recruit the interview participants. Noy (2008) defines this commonly used method as a sampling procedure in which the researcher accesses informants through contact information provided by other informants. Hans, the campus pastor of the southwest location of WWC, served as the primary recruiter for interviews and helped facilitate initial contact between the researchers and the interview participants. Once contact was made with potential interview participants, "Explanation of Research" and "Pre-Interview Questionnaire" documents were electronically forwarded to those participants. Once participation in the research was confirmed, an interview was scheduled and the completed pre-interview questionnaire was either returned electronically or brought to the interview.

Interviews are important in that they allow for the deepest exploration of individual interpretations of the issue being studied (Weiss 1994). These interpretations are often very nuanced, especially when it comes to racial ideology. The average interview time was 58.34 minutes, with seven interviews occurring in-person in private locations and twelve occurring via the telephone. All interviews were audio recorded and transcribed using pseudonyms to ensure participant confidentiality. These pseudonyms were chosen by the interview participants. Audio recording interviews is a common practice because it allows the interviewer to be fully present while interviewing. We conducted the interviews utilizing a semistructured and open-ended format, which creates opportunities for themes to emerge (Lofland et al. 2006). We also collected field notes during the interviews, which is important for capturing elements (e.g., attire, facial expressions, emotion, environment, etc.) of the interview process that may not be evident in the transcripts (Emerson, Fretz, and Shaw 1995).

Our interview protocol is an adaptation of Eduardo Bonilla-Silva's (2006) interview protocol printed in the second of *Racism without Racists*. Although the protocol is different from that of Bonilla-Silva, we chose it as a foundation because like our research, it seeks to understand racial ideologies and how racism can be reproduced through a critical lens. Bonilla-Silva's interview protocol had about ten main sections, including: background information; school socialization; employment, home, and school information; romantic life; overall minority views; racism and life chances; government intervention and minorities; reverse discrimination; job competition; and crime. For our interview protocol, we kept similar features—five main sections with multiple questions and follow-ups for each. There are also some distinguishable differences. First, instead of having a section on background, we developed the pre-interview questionnaire that covered the participant's church involvement, whether or not they considered wwc to be multiracial, and participant demographics, including age and race. The first two sections (Church Information and Racial/Ethnic Identity) ask additional and more open-ended questions in regards to the participant's background. Second, we divided the section on racism into two sections: "Racism" and "Racism & Church," followed by the "Conclusion" section. In the section titled "Racism," we asked participants how they defined racism, if organizations could be considered racist, and if the election of President Obama signaled that the United States was a postracial society. In the section titled "Racism and Church," we asked participants how important racial equality was to their Christian values and followed this with a series of questions seeking to understand how certain racialized events were framed, if at all, by members of the congregation. Specifically, we asked about the 2016 U.S. presidential election, the August 12, 2017, Unite the Right rally in Charlottesville, NFL protests, and the death of George Floyd Jr. Following these questions, we also asked if participants witnessed or experienced racism at wwc, how they would describe wwc's commitment to racial equality, and their view of wwc's commitment to eliminating racial inequalities.

Critical Ethnography

We utilized a critical ethnographic methodology to collect and analyze interview and participant observation data. Jim Thomas (1993, 4) defines critical ethnography as the "reflective process of choosing between conceptual alternatives and making value-laden judgments of meaning and method to challenge research, policy, and other forms of human activity." It is the reflective component of this definition that forms the distinction between conventional and critical ethnography. Critical ethnography goes beyond the question, "What is this?" by asking, "What could this be?" In asking these questions, critical ethnographers describe, analyze, and scrutinize hidden agendas, power centers, and assumptions that inhibit, repress, and constrain. In other words, critical ethnography is conventional ethnography with a political purpose (Thomas 1993). The political nature of critical ethnography means its practitioners seek social change by speaking on behalf of marginalized groups, in an effort to give more agency and authority to those voices. Critical ethnography is also emancipatory in that it seeks to negate repressive influences that lead to social domination of groups in order to bring about greater freedom and equity (Thomas 1993; Madison 2012). We utilized this strategy in studying the WWC case in order to go beneath the surface and examine the ways in which racism and White supremacy may be reproduced through seemingly innocent or color-blind methods.

All interview data were transcribed through an online transcription service that uses human professionals. Once the data were transcribed, we reviewed for accuracy. We made multiple edits, including inserting pseudonyms and correcting misspellings. When necessary, we added ellipses, italics, and capital letters to add emphasis. Although we did not transcribe the data, we did want the data to mirror the responses of participants as closely as possible. This was especially important considering Bonilla-Silva's (2018) notion of rhetorical incoherence. Over the course of this book, when presenting direct quotes, we sometimes took words out in order to reduce the lengths of quotes; however, we made sure that we did not change the meaning of the quote in any way.

As it relates to the analysis of the transcribed data, we utilized the qualitative software NVivo. We employed a multiple-stage coding process, following a constructivist grounded theory approach (Charmaz 2014; Corbin and Strauss 2008). This process allowed for themes and patterns to emerge. We especially looked for instances of Bonilla-Silva's color-blind racist frames (abstract liberalism, naturalization, minimization of race, and cultural racism) as well as styling (semantic moves, projection, stories, and rhetorical incoherence). We further looked for examples related to Victor Ray's (2019) racialized organizations theory (agency, distribution of resources, racialization and credentialing, and decoupling). We explored the data for new categories consistent with a constructivist approach. Subsequent rounds of coding were more focused on taking developed themes and superimposing them on all the transcripts. After ascertaining patterns in the coding, we sifted through the data again, looking for either confirmatory or contradictory examples for these emerging patterns. This allowed for further refinement of the data. From this, highly saturated codes formed the categories from which theories emerged.

Critical Discourse Analysis (CDA)

In order to understand the reproduction of racism through minimization of race and racism as well as the framing of racialized events, we employed a CDA when examining WWC's website and social media, including Twitter, YouTube, Facebook, and Instagram. We believe communications examined to be posted as formal documents representing the views of the church; thus, CDA was an appropriate analytical strategy. Faircloth (2013) defines CDA as the bringing together of the critical tradition of social analysis into language studies, which contributes to critical social analysis a particular focus on discourse and on relations between discourse and other social elements. These elements include power relations, ideologies, institutions, social identities, and so on. This analysis focuses on both the transparent and hidden ways in which domination, discrimination, and power manifests themselves in language and social interaction. Although there have been strides to incorporate visual images into concepts of discourse, the general bias of CDA is toward linguistically defined text concepts and structures, mostly applied to political, economic, and institutional discourse, ideology, racism, advertisement and promotional culture, media language, gender, education, and literacy (Blommaert and Bulcaen 2000). In short, CDA provides the appropriate methodological framework to analyze racism and the power dynamics revealed throughout discourse.

NOTES

Introduction

1. The term "evangelical" refers to a wide swath of conservative Christians. Emerson and Smith (2000) outline important evangelical beliefs and characteristics: the Bible as the final authority; the belief that Christ died for the salvation of all and that the acceptance of Christ (being born again) leads to eternal life; the importance of sharing the faith (evangelizing); self-identify as evangelical; 90 percent White; belief in "engaged orthodoxy."

2. Gary Alan Fine (2012, 4.2), a sociologist from Northwestern University, posed that "meso-level" refers to the "space between individual interaction and that of large-scale organizations and institutions: not untethered behavior, but the interaction order."

3. Despite the relatively low number of multiracial congregations in the United States, there is a growing body of literature studying multiracial churches. The terms "multicultural," "multiracial," "multiethnic," and "interracial" are often used interchangeably. While culture, race, and ethnicity are certainly not synonymous in the sociological literature, those in the pews often use these terms as if they were (Garces-Foley 2007a, 2007b). For the purposes of this work, multiracial will be the preferred terminology.

4. Exploring the reproduction of racism in a religiously multiracial context is important for multiple reasons. First, multiracial churches are growing in number and are now the fastest growing types of large Christian churches in the U.S. (Yancey 2000). This is due in part to the perceived power of these organizations to reduce racial divisions (DeYoung et al. 2003). This presupposes the idea that individuals are intentionally engaging in these spaces in order to build relationships and work with others of varying racial identities. Also, there is evidence that multiracial congregations have the ability to help individuals transcend racial and ethnic differences (Marti 2005, 2009). Secondly, in an era where the movement for Black lives has called attention to all facets of institutional racism, multiracial congregations not only helps people transcend race but also brings them together in pursuit of racial justice, equity and equality. The findings from this book as well as the work of the social science community, is necessary to understand the barriers and obstacles which may prevent this from happening.

5. The U.S. Census Bureau authorizes the use of "Latino" and "Hispanic" interchangeably as ethnic identifiers (U.S. Census Bureau 2013). I prefer to use the term Latinx as an acknowledg-

ment of current trends in both scholarship and society, especially in regards to gender neutral language. When speaking about specific individuals, I use more traditional language (Latino/Latina) based on the individual's self-identified gender assignment.

6. Hans is a fictitious name chosen at the discretion of the interview participant, as are the other names of interviewees in this volume. See chapter 3 for more information.

Chapter 2. Color-Blind Ideology and the Reproduction of Racism

1. Although we present each frame individually as well as provide examples, it is important to make two notations. First, these frames are often used in combination with each other and instances of this are commonly found in literature (Carter and Lippard 2020; Carter and Lippard 2015; Carter, Lippard, and Baird 2019). In these instances, we will attempt to demonstrate how the two frames are being used in tandem. Secondly, it is also important to note that while we provide examples for each frame, it is not an exhausting chronicling of all the examples we gathered of how each frame was used. Throughout, we made a concerted effort to let the data speak for itself.

REFERENCES

Acker, Joan. 1990. "A Theory of Gendered Organizations." *Gender and Society* 4:139–158.
Adams, James. 1965. "Inequity in Social Exchange." Pp. 267–299 in *Advances in Experimental Social Psychology*, vol. 2, edited by Leonard Berkowitz. New York: Academic Press.
Adorno, Theodor, Elise Frenkel-Brunswik, Daniel Levinson, and R. Sanford. 1950. *The Authoritarian Personality*. New York: Norton.
Aho, James. 2013. "Christian Heroism and the Reconstruction of America." *Critical Sociology* 39:545–60.
Alba, Richard. 1990. *Ethnic Identity: The Transformation of White America*. New Haven, Conn.: Yale University Press.
Allen, Theodore. 1994. *The Invention of the White Race*. Vol. 2, *The Origin of Racial Oppression in Anglo-America*. New York: Verso.
Allport, Gordon. 1950. *The Individual and His Religion*. New York: Macmillan.
———. 1954. *The Nature of Prejudice*. Cambridge, Mass.: Addison-Wesley.
Alumkal, Antony. 2001. "Being Korean, Being Christian: Particularism and Universalism in a Second-Generation Congregation." Pp. 181–192 in *Korean Americans and Their Religions: Pilgrims and Missionaries from a Different Shore*, edited by Ho Youn Kwon, Kwang Chung Kim, and R. Stephen Warner. University Park: Pennsylvania State University Press.
———. 2005. *Asian American Evangelical Churches: Race, Ethnicity, and Assimilation in the Second Generation*. New York: LFB Scholarly Publishing.
Ammerman, Nancy, with Arthur E. Farnsley II and Tammy Adams et al. 1997. *Congregations and Community*. New Brunswick, N.J.: Rutgers University Press.
Anderson, Monica. 2015. "A Rising Share of the U.S. Black Population Is Foreign Born: 9 Percent Are Immigrants; and While Most Are from the Caribbean, Africans Drive Recent Growth." Pew Research Center, Washington D.C., April 9, 2015. https://www.pewresearch.org/social-trends/2015/04/09/a-rising-share-of-the-u-s-black-population-is-foreign-born/.
Austin, William, and Elaine Walster. 1980. "Reactions to Confirmations and Disconfirmations of Expectancies of Equity and Inequity." *Journal of Personality and Social Psychology* 16:426–441.

Awad, Germaine, Kevin Cokley, and Joseph Ravitch. 2005. "Attitudes toward Affirmative Action: A Comparison of Color-Blind versus Modern Racist Attitudes." *Journal of Applied Social Psychology* 35(7):1384–1399.

Bailey, Benjamin. 2001. "Dominican-American Ethnic/Racial Identities and United States Social Categories." *International Migration Review* 35:667–708.

Baker, Joseph, Samuel Perry, and Andrew Whitehead. 2020. "Keep America Christian (and White): Christian Nationalism, Fear of Ethnoracial Outsiders, and Intention to Vote for Donald Trump in the 2020 Presidential Election." *Sociology of Religion* 81(3):272–293.

Balmer, Randall. 2017. "Under Trump, Evangelicals Show Their True Racist Colors." *Los Angeles Times*, August 23. http://www.latimes.com/opinion/op-ed/la-oe-balmer-evangelical-trump-racism-20170823-story.html.

Barr, Simone C., and Helen A. Neville. 2008. "Examination of the Link between Parental Racial Socialization Messages and Racial Ideology among Black College Students." *Journal of Black Psychology* 34(2):131–155.

Barron, Jessica. 2016. "Managed Diversity: Race, Place and an Urban Church." *Sociology of Religion* 17(1):18–36.

Becker, Penny. 1999. *Congregations in Conflict: Cultural Models of Local Religious Life*. Cambridge: Cambridge University Press.

Bell, Carl. 2004. "Racism: A Mental Illness?" *Psychiatric Services* 55(12):1343.

Bell, Michael, and Douglas Hartmann. 2007. "Diversity in Everyday Discourse: The Cultural Ambiguities and Consequences of 'Happy Talk.'" *Critical Sociology* 72:895.

Bernard, H. Russell. 1994. *Research Methods in Anthropology: Qualitative and Quantitative Approaches*. 2nd ed. Walnut Creek, Calif.: AltaMira Press.

Berrey, Ellen. 2011. "Why Diversity Became Orthodox in Higher Education, and How It Changed the Meaning of Race on Campus." *Critical Sociology* 35:573–96.

Bertrand, Marianne, and Sendhil Mullainathan. 2004. "Are Emily and Greg More Employable than Lakisha and Jamal? A Field Experiment on Labor Market Discrimination." *American Economic Review* 94(4):991–1013.

Blanchard, Troy. 2007. "Conservative Protestant Congregations and Racial Residential Segregation: Evaluating the Closed Community Thesis in Metropolitan and Nonmetropolitan Counties." *American Sociological Review* 72:416–433.

Blank, Rebecca. 2001. "An Overview of Trends in Social and Economic Well-being, by Race." Pp. 21–39 in *American Becoming: Racial Trends and Their Consequences*, vol. 1, edited by Neil Smelser, William Wilson, and Faith Mitchell. Washington, D.C.: National Academy Press.

Blau, Judith. 2003. *Race in the Schools: Perpetuating White Dominance?* Boulder, Colo.: Lynne Rienner.

Blommaert, Jan, and Chris Bulcaen. 2000. "Critical Discourse Analysis." *Annual Review of Anthropology* 29(1):447–466.

Blumer, Herbert. 1958. "Race Prejudice as a Sense of Group Position." *Pacific Sociological Review* 1:3–7.

Blumhofer, Edith. 2006. "Azusa Street Revival." *Christian Century* 123(5): 20–22.

Bobo, Lawrence, and James Kluegel. 1997. "Status, Ideology, and Dimensions of Whites' Racial Beliefs and Attitudes: Progress and Stagnation." Pp. 93–120 in *Racial Attitudes in the 1990s: Continuity and Change*, edited by Steven Tuch and Jack Martin. Westport, Conn.: Praeger.

Bobo, Lawrence, and Mia Tuan. 2006. *Prejudice in Politics: Group Position, Public Opinion, and the Wisconsin Treaty Rights Dispute*. Cambridge, Mass.: Harvard University Press.

Boles, John. 1988. *Masters and Slaves in the House of the Lord: Race and Religion in the American South, 1740–1870*. Lexington: University Press of Kentucky.

Bonilla-Silva. 1997. "Rethinking Racism: Toward a Structural Interpretation." *American Sociological Review* 62(3):465–480.

———. 2003. *Racism without Racists: Color-Blind Racism and the Persistence of Racial Inequality in America*. Lanham, Md.: Rowman and Littlefield.

———. 2006. *Racism without Racists: Color-Blind Racism and the Persistence of Racial Inequality in the United States*. 2nd ed. Lanham, Md.: Rowman & Littlefield.

———. 2018. *Racism without Racists: Color-Blind Racism and the Persistence of Racial Inequality in America*. Lanham, Md.: Rowman and Littlefield.

Bonilla-Silva, Eduardo, and David Dietrich. 2011. "The Sweet Enchantment of Color-Blind Racism in Obamerica." *Annals of the American Academy of Political and Social Science* 634(1):190–206.

Boston, Rob. 2017. "In Their Responses to Charlottesville, Trump and His Religious Right Allies Failed a Simple Moral Test." *Americans United for Separation of Church and State*. https://www.au.org/blogs/wall-of-separation/in-their-responses-to-charlottesville-trump-and-his-religious-right-allies.

Braunstein, Ruth. 2017. "Muslims as Outsiders, Enemies, and Others: The 2016 Presidential Election and the Politics of Religious Exclusion." *American Journal of Cultural Sociology* 5(3):355–372.

Buchanan, Larry, Quoctrung Bui, and Jugal Patel. 2020. "Black Lives Matter Maybe the Largest Movement in U.S. History." *New York Times*, July 3. https://www.nytimes.com/interactive/2020/07/03/us/george-floyd-protests-crowd-size.html.

Bulman, Ronnie, and Camille Wortman. 1977. "Attributions of Blame and Coping in the 'Real World': Severe Accident Victims React to Their Lot." *Journal of Personality and Social Psychology* 35(5):351–363.

Burke, Meghan A. 2016. "New Frontiers in the Study of Color-Blind Racism: A Materialist Approach." *Social Currents* 3(2):103–109.

Burris, Christopher, and Lynne Jackson. 2000. "Social Identity and the True Believer: Responses to Threatened Self-Stereotypes among the Intrinsically Religious." *British Journal of Social Psychology* 39:257–278.

Calhoun-Brown, Allison. 2000. "Upon this Rock: The Black Church, Nonviolence, and the Civil Rights Movement." *PS: Political Science and Politics* 33(2):169–174.

Carrillo, Ian. 2021. "Racialized Organizations and Color-Blind Racial Ideology in Brazil." *Sociology of Race and Ethnicity* 7(1):56–70.

Carter, J. Scott, and Shannon K. Carter. 2014. "Place Matters: The Impact of Place of Residency on Racial Attitudes among Regional and Urban Migrants." *Social Science Research* 47:165–177.

———. 2017. "Boundary Blurring? The Declining Significance of Place on Whites' Attitudes toward Affirmative Action." *Southern Studies* 24:27–52.

Carter, J. Scott, and Mamadi Corra. 2005. "Changing Attitudes toward Women, 1972–1998: The Liberalization of Religious Fundamentalists." *Michigan Sociological Review* 19:19–44.

———. 2012. "Beliefs about the Causes of Racial Inequality: The Persisting Impact of Urban and Suburban Locations?" *Urban Studies Research*.

———. 2016. "Racial Resentment and Attitudes toward the Use of Force among Whites: An Over-Time Trend Analysis." *Sociological Inquiry* 86:492–511.

Carter, J. Scott, Mamadi Corra, Shannon K. Carter, and Rachel McCrosky. 2014. "The Impact of Place? A Reassessment of the Importance of the South in Affecting Beliefs about Racial Inequality." *Social Science Journal* 51:12–20.

Carter, J. Scott, Mamadi Corra, and David Jenks. 2016. "In the Shadows of Ferguson: The Role of Racial Resentment on White Attitudes toward the Use of Force by Police." *International Journal of Criminal Justice Sciences* 11:114–131.

Carter, J. Scott, and Cameron Lippard. 2015. "Group Position, Threat, and Immigration: The Role of Interest Groups and Elite Actors in Setting the 'Lines of Discussion.'" *Sociology of Race and Ethnicity* 1(3):394–408.

———. 2020. *The Death of Affirmative Action? Racialized Framing and the Fight against Racial Preference in College Admissions*. Bristol: Bristol University Press.

Carter, J. Scott, Cameron Lippard, and Andrew Baird. 2019. "Veiled Threats: Color-Blind Frames and Group Threat in Affirmative Action Discourse." *Social Problems* 66(4):503–518.

Carter, J. Scott, Lala Steelman, Lynn Mulkey, and Casey Borch. 2005. "When the Rubber Meets the Road: The Differential Effects of Urbanism and Region on Principle and Implementation Measures of Racial Tolerance." *Social Science Research* 34:408–425.

Charmaz, Kathy. 2014. *Constructing Grounded Theory*. 2nd ed. Thousand Oaks, Calif.: Sage.

Chaves, Mark. 1998. *National Congregations Study: Data File and Codebook*. Tucson: University of Arizona.

———. 2004. *Congregations in America*. Cambridge, Mass.: Harvard University Press.

Chaves, Mark, Mary Ellen Konieczny, Kraig Beyerlein, and Emily Barman. 1999. "The National Congregations Study: Background, Methods, and Selected Results." *Journal for the Scientific Study of Religion* 38:458–476.

Choi, Kate, Arthur Sakamoto, and Daniel Powers. 2008. "Who Is Hispanic? Hispanic Identity among African Americans, Asian Americans, Others and Whites." *Sociological Inquiry* 78(3):335–371.

Christerson, Brad, Korie Edwards, and Michael Emerson. 2005. *Against All Odds: The Struggle for Racial Integration in Religious Organizations*. New York: New York University Press.

Christerson, Brad, and Michael Emerson. 2003. "The Costs of Diversity in Religious Organizations: An In-Depth Case Study." *Sociology of Religion* 64(2):163–181.

Cobb, Ryon J., Samuel L. Perry, and Kevin D. Dougherty. 2015. "United by Faith? Race/Ethnicity, Congregational Diversity, and Explanations of Racial Inequality." *Sociology of Religion* 76(2):177–198.

Collins, Patricia Hill. 1990. *Black Feminist Thought: Knowledge, Consciousness, and the Politics of Empowerment*. 2nd ed. Boston: Unwin Hyman.

———. 2000. *Fighting Words*. Minneapolis: University of Minnesota Press.

Collins, Sharon. 2011. "From Affirmative Action to Diversity: Erasing Inequality from Organizational Responsibility." *Critical Sociology* 37:517–520.

Corbin, Juliet, and Anselm Strauss. 2008. *Basics of Qualitative Research*. 3rd ed. Los Angeles: Sage.

References

Cornell, Stephen, and Douglas Hartmann. 1998. *Ethnicity and Race: Making Identities in a Changing World*. Thousand Oaks, Calif.: Pine Forge Press.

Corra, Mamadi, and J. Scott Carter. 2008. "Shadow of the Past?: Assessing Racial and Gender Differences in Confidence in the Institutions of Science and Medicine." *Black Women, Gender, and Families* 2(1):54–83.

Council of Economic Advisors. 1998. *Changing America: Indicators of Social and Economic Well-Being by Race and Hispanic Origin*. Washington, D.C.: Author.

Cox, Jonathan. 2021. "When Color-Conscious Meets Color-Blind: Millennials of Color and Color-Blind Racism." *Sociological Inquiry* 92:769–791.

Crosby, Faye, and A. Miren Gonzalez-Intal. 1984. "Relative Deprivation and Equity Theories." Pp. 141–166 in *The Sense of Injustice: Social Psychological Perspectives*, edited by Robert Folger. Boston: Springer.

Cross, William, Jr. 1971. "The Negro-to-Black Conversion Experience." *Black World* 20(9):13–27.

Dahab, Ramsey, and Marisa Omori. 2019. "Homegrown Foreigners: How Christian Nationalism and Nativist Attitudes Impact Muslim Civil Liberties." *Racial and Ethnic Studies* 42(10):1727–1746.

Davis, Joshua. 2018. "Enforcing Christian Nationalism: Examining the Link between Group Identity and Punitive Attitudes in the United States." *Journal for the Scientific Study of Religion* 57(2):300–317.

Davis, Joshua, and Samuel Perry. 2020. "White Christian Nationalism and Relative Political Tolerance for Racists." *Social Problems* 68(3):513–534.

Demo, David, and Michael Hughes. 1991. "Socialization and Racial Identity among Black Americans." *Social Psychology Quarterly* 53(4):364–374.

Devos, Thierry, and Mahzarin Banaji. 2005. "American = White?" *Journal of Personality and Social Psychology* 88(3):447–466.

DeYoung, Curtiss, Michael Emerson, George Yancey, and Karen Kim. 2003. *United by Faith: The Multiracial Congregation as an Answer to the Problem of Race*. New York: Oxford University Press.

Dhingra, Pawan. 2007. *Managing Multicultural Lives: Asian American Professionals and the Challenge of Multiple Identities*. Stanford, Calif.: Stanford University Press.

Doane, Ashley. 1997. "Dominant Group Ethnic Identity in the United States: The Role of 'Hidden' Ethnicity in Intergroup Relations." *Sociological Quarterly* 38(3):375–397.

———. 2003. "Rethinking Whiteness Studies." Pp. 1–27 in *White Out: The Continuing Significance of Racism*, edited by Ashley Doane and Eduardo Bonilla-Silva. New York: Routledge.

———. 2006. "What Is Racism: Racial Discourse and Racial Politics." *Critical Sociology* 32(2–3):255–274.

———. 2017. "Beyond Color-Blindness: (Re)theorizing Racial Ideology." *Sociological Perspectives* 60(5):975–991.

———. 2020. "Post-Colorblindness?: Trump and the Rise of the New White Nationalism." Pp. 27–42 in Lippard, Carter, and Embrick, *Protecting Whiteness*.

Doggett, Jolie. 2015. "5 Code Words the Media Needs to Stop Using to Describe Black People. *Essence*, April 29. https://www.essence.com/news/5-code-words-media-needs-stop-using-describe-black-people/.

Dotson, Hillary, and J. Scott Carter. 2012. "Changing Views toward the Death Penalty? The Intersecting Impact of Race and Gender on Attitudes, 1974–2006." *Justice System Journal* 33:1–21.

Dougherty, Kevin. 2003. "How Monochromatic Is Church Membership? Racial-Ethnic Diversity in Religious Community." *Sociology of Religion* 64:65–85.

Dougherty, Kevin D., Mark Chaves, and Michael O. Emerson. 2020. "Racial Diversity in U.S. Congregations, 1998–2019." *Journal for the Scientific Study of Religion* 59(4):651–662.

Dougherty, Kevin, and Kimberly Huyser. 2008. "Racially Diverse Congregations: Organizational Identity and the Accommodation of Differences." *Journal for the Scientific Study of Religion* 47(1):23–43.

Dougherty, Kevin, Byron Johnson, and Edward Polson. 2007. "Recovering the Lost: Remeasuring U.S. Religious Affiliation." *Journal for the Scientific Study of Religion* 46:483–499.

Dougherty, Kevin, Gerardo Marti, and Brandon Martinez. 2015. "Congregational Diversity and Attendance in a Mainline Protestant Denomination." *Journal for the Scientific Study of Religion* 54(4):668–683.

Douglas, Karen, Rogelio Saenz, and Aurelia Murga. 2015. "Immigration in the Era of Color-Blind Racism." *American Behavioral Scientist* 59(11):1429–1451.

Dovidio, Jack, and Sam Gaertner. 2005. "Color Blind or Just Plain Blind? The Pernicious Nature of Contemporary Racism." *Nonprofit Quarterly*, June 21. https://nonprofitquarterly.org/understanding-new-racism-bias/.

Dovidio, John, Samuel Gaertner, and Tamar Saguy. 2015. "Color-Blindness and Commonality: Included but Invisible?" *American Behavioral Scientist* 59(11):1518–1538.

Driskill, Gerald, Alexandra Arjannikova, and John Meyer. 2014. "A Dialectic Analysis of a Community Forum on Faith: The 'Most Segregated' or 'Separated Hour?'" *Journal of Applied Communication Research* 42(4):477–496.

DuBois, William. 1935. *Black Reconstruction in America: An Essay toward a History of the Part which Black Folk Played in the Attempt to Reconstruct Democracy in America, 1860–1880*. New York: Russell and Russell.

Durr, Marlese. 2020. "Echoing Derrick A. Bell: Black Women's Resistance to White Supremacy in the Age of Trump." Pp. 224–239 in Lippard, Carter, and Embrick, *Protecting Whiteness*.

Edgell, Penny, and Eric Tranby. 2010. "Shared Visions? Diversity and Cultural Membership in American Life." *Social Problems* 57(2):175–204.

Edwards, Korie. 2008a. "Bring Race to the Center: The Importance of Race in Racially Diverse Religious Organizations." *Journal for the Scientific Study of Religion* 47(1):5–9.

———. 2008b. *The Elusive Dream: The Power of Race in Interracial Churches*. New York: Oxford University Press.

———. 2014. "Role Strain Theory and Understanding the Role of Head Clergy of Racially Diverse Churches." *Sociology of Religion* 75(1):57–79.

Ekins, Emily. 2017. "The Five Types of Trump Voters: Who They Are and What They Believe." Report, Democracy Fund Voter Study Group.

Elliott, Josh. 2020. "Outrage Erupts over 'Karen' Who Called Cops on Black Birdwatcher in Central Park." *Global News*, May 26. https://globalnews.ca/news/6986111/central-park-karen-amy-cooper-dog/.

Embrick, David. 2011. "The Diversity Ideology in the Business World: A New Oppression for a New Age." *Critical Sociology* 37:541–556.

Embrick, David, J. Scott Carter, and Cameron Lippard. 2020. "The Resurgence of Whitelash: White Supremacy, Resistance, and the Racialized Social System in Trumptopia." Pp. 3–23, in Lippard, Carter, and Embrick, *Protecting Whiteness*.

Embrick, David G., J. Scott Carter, Cameron Lippard, and Bhoomi K. Thakore. 2020. "Capitalism, Racism, and Trumpism: Whitelash and the Politics of Oppression." *Fast Capitalism* 17(1):203–224.

Embrick, David, Simon Weffer, and Silvia Dominguez. 2019. "White Sanctuaries: Race and Place in Art Museums." *International Journal of Sociology and Social Policy* 39(11/12):995–1009.

Emerson, Michael. 2006. *People of the Dream: Multiracial Congregations in the United States*. New York: Oxford University Press.

———. 2010. "Who's Succeeding at Making Churches More Multiracial?" In *God's Politics* (blog), February 2. https://sojo.net/articles/whos-succeeding-making-churches-more-multiracial.

Emerson, Michael, and Karen Chai Kim. 2018. "Multiracial Congregations: An Analysis of Their Development and a Typology." *Journal for the Scientific Study of Religion* 42(2):217–227.

Emerson, Michael, and Christian Smith. 2000. *Divided by Faith: Evangelical Religion and the Problem of Race in America*. New York: Oxford University Press.

Emerson, Michael, and George Yancey. 2008. "African Americans in Interracial Congregations an Analysis of Demographics, Social Networks, and Social Attitudes." *Review of Religious Research* 49(3):301–318.

Faircloth, Norman. 2013. *Critical Discourse Analysis*. London: Routledge.

Feagin, Joe. 2013. *The White Racial Frame: Centuries of Racial Framing and Counter-Framing*. 2nd ed. New York: Routledge.

Fields, Barbara. 1990. "Slavery, Race, and Ideology in the United States of America." *New Left Review* 181(1):95–118.

Fine, Gary Alan. 2012. "Group Culture and the Interaction Order: Local Sociology on the Meso-Level." *Annual Review of Sociology* 38:159–179.

Frankenberg, Ruth. 1993. *White Women, Race Matters: The Social Construction of Whiteness*. Minneapolis: University of Minnesota Press.

Gallagher, Charles. 1997. "Redefining Racial Privilege in the United States." *Transformations: The Journal of Inclusive Scholarship and Pedagogy* 8(1):28–39.

———. 2020. "Institutional Racism Revisited: How Institutions Perpetuate and Promote Racism through Color Blindness." Pp. 89–101 in Lippard, Carter, and Embrick, *Protecting Whiteness*.

Gans, Herbert. 1979. "Symbolic Ethnicity: The Future of Ethnic Groups in America." *Ethnic and Racial Studies* 2(1):1–20.

Garces-Foley, Kathleen. 2007a. *Crossing the Ethnic Divide: The Multiethnic Church on a Mission*. New York: Oxford University Press.

———. 2007b. "New Opportunities and New Values: The Emergence of the Multicultural Church." *Annals of the American Academy of Political and Social Science* 612(1):209–224.

Goldberg, Michelle. 2006. *Kingdom Coming: The Rise of Christian Nationalism*. New York: W. W. Norton.

Gorski, Philip. 2009. "Conservative Protestantism in the United States: Toward a Comparative Historical Perspective." Pp. 74–114 in *Evangelicals and Democracy in America*, 1, edited by Steven Brint and Jean Schroedel. New York: Russell Sage.

———. 2017a. "Reviving the Civil Religious Tradition." Pp. 269–288 in *Religion and Progressive Activism: New Stories about Faith and Politics*, edited by Ruth Braunstein, Nicholas Fuist, Rhys H. Williams, and Rhys H. Williams. New York: New York University Press.

———. 2017b. "Why Evangelicals Voted for Trump: A Critical Cultural Sociology." *American Journal of Cultural Sociology* 5(3):338–354.

Gourley, Bruce. 2015. *Crucible of Faith and Freedom: Baptists and the American Civil War*. Macon, Ga.: Nurturing Faith.

Grazian, David. 2004. *Blue Chicago: The Search for Authenticity in Urban Blues Clubs*. Chicago: University of Chicago Press.

Hardiman, Rita. 1994. "White Racial Identity Development in the United States." Pp. 117–136 in *Race, Ethnicity, and Self: Identity in Multicultural Perspective*, edited by Elizabeth Salett and Diane Koslow. Washington, D.C.: National Multicultural Institute.

Hardiman, Rita, and Molly Keehn. 2012. "White Identity Development Revisited: Listening to White Students." Pp. 121–137 in *New Perspectives on Racial Identity Development: Integrating Emerging Frameworks*, 2nd ed., edited by Charmaine Wijeyesinghe and Bailey Jackson III. New York: New York University Press.

Harris, Cherly. 1993. "Whiteness as Property." *Harvard Law Review* 106:1707– 1791.

Hatch, Nathan. 1989. *The Democratization of American Christianity*. New Haven, Conn.: Yale University Press.

Hawkins, Darnell. 2001. "Commentary on Randall Kennedy's Overview of the Justice System." Pp. 32–51 in *America Becoming: Racial Trends and Their Consequences*, vol. 2, edited by Neil Smelser, William Wilson, and Faith Mitchell. Washington, D.C.: National Academy Press.

Helms, Janet. 1990. *Black and White Racial Identity: Theory, Research, and Practice*. New York: Greenwood Press.

———. 1993. "I Also Said, 'White Racial Identity Influences White Researchers.'" *Counseling Psychologist* 21(2):240–243.

Hessekiel, David. 2020. "Companies Taking a Public Stand in the Wake of George Floyd's Death." *Forbes*, June 4. https://www.forbes.com/sites/davidhessekiel/2020/06/04/companies-taking-a-public-stand-in-the-wake-of-george-floyds-death/?sh=65dd64da7214.

Hill, Deborah, David Matz, and Wendy Wood. 2010. "Why Don't We Practice What We Preach? A Meta-Analytic Review of Religious Racism." *Personality and Social Psychology Review* 14(1):126–139.

Howard, Judith. 2000. "Social Psychology of Identities." *Annual Review of Sociology* 26:367–393.

Hughes, Philip. 2017. "Theology and social sciences in ministry research." *Journal of Contemporary Ministry* 3:37–57.

Humes, Karen, Nicholas Jones, and Roberto Ramirez. 2011. "Overview of Race and Hispanic Origin: 2010 Census Briefs." United States Census Bureau.

Hunt, Matthew, and Rashawn Ray. 2012. "Social Class Identification among Black Americans: Trends and Determinants, 1974–2010." *American Behavioral Scientist* 56:1462–1480.

Hutchinson, Janis, Nestor Rodriguez, and Jacqueline Hagan. 1996. "Community Life: African Americans in Multiethnic Residential Areas." *Journal of Black Studies* 27(2):201–223.

Ince, Jelani. 2022. "'Saved' by Interaction, Living by Race: The Diversity Demeanor in an Organizational Space." *Social Psychology Quarterly* 85(3):259–278.

Inwood, Joshua. 2015. "Neoliberal Racism: The 'Southern Strategy' and the Expanding Geographies of White Supremacy." *Social and Cultural Geography* 16(4):407–423.

Irving, S. 1973. "Racial Attitudes of American Ministers." Paper presented at the 81st annual meeting of the American Psychological Association, Montreal.

Itzigsohn, José, Silvia Giorguli, and Obed Vazquez. 2005. "Immigrant Incorporation and Racial Identity: Racial Self-Identification among Dominican Immigrants." *Ethnic and Racial Studies* 28(1):50–78.

Jackson, Lynne, and Bruce Hunsberger. 1999. "An Intergroup Perspective on Religion and Prejudice." *Journal for the Scientific Study of Religion* 38:509–523.

Jenkins, J. Jacob, and Patrick Dillon. 2012. "This Is What We're All About: The (Re)construction of an Oppressive Organizational Structure." *Southern Communication Journal* 77:287–306.

Jeung, Russell. 2004. *Faithful Generations: Race and New Asian American Churches*. New Brunswick, N.J.: Rutgers University Press.

Johnson, Bryan, and Cardell Jacobson. 2005. "Contact in Context: An Examination of Social Settings on Whites' Attitudes toward Interracial Marriage." *Social Psychology Quarterly* 68(4):387–399.

Joiner, L. 2004. "The State of Black Health." *Crisis* 111(6):17–27.

Jones, J. M. 2021. "The Dual Pandemics of COVID-19 and Systemic Racism: Navigating Our Path Forward." *School Psychology* 26(5):427–431.

Jones, Robert. 2020. *White Too Long: The Legacy of White Supremacy in American Christianity*. New York: Simon & Schuster.

Jones, Jo, and William D. Mosher. 2013. "Fathers' Involvement with Their Children: United States, 2006–2010." *National Health Statistics Reports*, no. 71. https://www.cdc.gov/nchs/data/nhsr/nhsr071.pdf.

Kanter, Rosabeth Moss. 1977. "Some Effects of Proportions on Group Life: Skewed Sex Ratios and Responses to Token Women." *American Journal of Sociology* 82:965–91.

Kibria, Nazli. 2000. "Race, Ethnic Options, and Ethnic Binds: Identity Negotiations for Second Generation Chinese and Korean Americans." *Sociological Perspectives* 43(1):77–95.

Kim, Rebecca. 2004. "Second-Generation Korean American Evangelicals: Ethnic, Multiethnic, or White Campus Ministries?" *Sociology of Religion* 65(1):19–34.

———. 2006. *God's New Whiz Kids? Korean American Evangelicals on Campus*. New York: New York University Press.

Kinder, Donald R., and Lynn M. Sanders. 1996. *Divided by Color: Racial Politics and Democratic Ideals*. Chicago: University of Chicago Press.

King, Martin, Jr. 1963. "I Have a Dream Speech." August 28, 1963, Washington, D.C. Available at https://www.history.com/topics/civil-rights-movement/i-have-a-dream-speech.

Lacy, Karyn. 2007. *Blue-Chip Black: Race, Class, and Status in the New Black Middle Class*. Berkeley: University of California Press.

Lati, Marisa. 2021. "What Is Critical Race Theory, and Why Do Republicans Want to Ban It in Schools?" *Washington Post*, May 29. https://www.washingtonpost.com/education/2021/05/29/critical-race-theory-bans-schools/.

Leacock, Eleanor, Martin Deutsch, and Joshua Fishman. 1959. "The Bridgeview Study: A Preliminary Report." *Journal of Social Issues* 15:30–37.

Leonardo, Zeus. 2004. "The Color of Supremacy: Beyond the Discourse of 'White Privilege.'" *Educational Philosophy and Theory* 36:137–152.

Lerner, Melvin. "The Justice Motive in Human Relations: Some Thoughts on what We Know and Need to Know about Justice." Pp. 11–35 in *The Justice Motive in Social Behavior*, edited by Melvin Lerner and Sally Lerner. New York: Academic.

Lincoln, Eric, and Lawrence Mamiya. 1990. *The Black Church in the African American Experience*. Durham, N.C.: Duke University Press.

Lippard, Cameron, J. Scott Carter, and David Embrick. 2020. *Protecting Whiteness: Whitelash and the Rejection of Racial Equality*. Seattle: University of Washington Press.

Lofland, John, David Snow, Leon Anderson, and Lyn Lofland. 2006. *Analyzing Social Settings: A Guide to Qualitative Observation and Analysis*. 4th ed. Belmont, Calif.: Wadsworth/Thomson Learning.

Logan, John, Weiwei Zhang, Richard Turner, and Allison Shertzer. 2015. "Creating the Black Ghetto: Black Residential Patterns Before and During the Great Migration." *Annals of the American Academy of Political and Social Science* 660(1):18–35.

Lunenburg, Fred. 2012. "Power and Leadership: An Influence Process." *International Journal of Management, Business, and Administration* 15(1):1–9.

Madison, A. Soyini. 2012. *Critical Ethnography: Methods, Ethics, and Performance*. 2nd ed. Los Angeles: Sage.

Major, Brenda. 1994. "From Social Inequality to Personal Entitlement: The Role of Social Comparisons, Legitimacy Appraisals, and Group Membership." *Advances in Experimental Social Psychology* 26:293–355.

Major, Brenda, Alison Blodorn, and Gregory Blascovich. 2018. "The Threat of Increasing Diversity: Why Many Americans Support Trump in the 2016 Presidential Election." *Group Processes & Intergroup Relations* 21(6):931–940.

Manis, Andrew. 1999. "Dying from the Neck Up: Southern Baptist Resistance to the Civil Rights Movement." *Baptist History and Heritage* 34(1):33–49.

———. 2020. "George Floyd and the Silence of White Evangelical America." *Baptist News Global*, June 3. https://baptistnews.com/article/george-floyd-and-white-evangelical-america/#.YEg4PiIh1pQ.

Manning, Alex, Douglas Hartmann, and Joseph Gerteis. 2015. "Colorblindness in Black and White: An Analysis of Core Tenets, Configurations, and Complexities." *Sociology of Race and Ethnicity* 1(4):532–546.

Marti, Gerardo. 2005. *A Mosaic of Believers: Diversity and Innovation in a Multiethnic Church*. Bloomington: Indiana University Press.

———. 2009. "Affinity, Identity, and Transcendence: The Experience of Religious Racial Integration in Diverse Congregations." *Journal for the Scientific Study of Religion* 48(1):53–68.

———. 2010. "The Religious Racial Integration of African Americans into Diverse Churches." *Journal for the Scientific Study of Religion* 49:201–207.

References

———. 2012. *Worship across the Racial Divide: Religious Music and the Multiracial Congregation.* New York: Oxford University Press.
Martin, Brian. 1986. "Suppression and Social Action." Pp. 257–263 in *Intellectual Suppression: Australian Case Histories, Analysis and Responses*, edited by Brian Martin, C. M. Ann Baker, Clyde Manwell, and Cedric Pugh. Sydney: Angus and Robertson.
Marty, Martin. 1990. "North America." Pp. 396–406 in *The Oxford History of Christianity*, edited by John McManners. Oxford: Oxford University Press.
Marvasti, Amir, and Karyn McKinney. 2011. "Does Diversity Mean Assimilation?" *Critical Sociology* 37:631–50.
Marx, Karl, and Friedrich Engels. 2011. "The German Ideology 1845." Pp. 161–171 in *Cultural Theory: An Anthology*, edited by Imre Szeman and Timothy Kaposy. Malden, Mass.: Wiley-Blackwell.
Mayorga-Gallo, Sarah. 2019. "The White-Centering Logic of Diversity Ideology." *American Behavioral Scientist* 63(13):1789–1809.
McDaniel, Eric, Irfan Nooruddin, and Allyson Shortle. 2011. "Divine Boundaries: How Religion Shapes Citizens' Attitudes toward Immigrants." *American Politics Research* 39:205–233.
McDermott, Monica, and Frank Samson. 2005. "White Racial and Ethnic Identity in the United States." *Annual Review of Sociology* 31:245–61.
McDonald, Maretta. 2020. "Blue Lives Matter: Police Protection or Countermovement." Pp. 210–223 in Lippard, Carter, and Embrick, *Protecting Whiteness*.
Merino, Stephen. 2010. "Religious Diversity in a 'Christian Nation': The Effects of Theological Exclusivity and Interreligious Contact on the Acceptance of Religious Diversity." *Journal for the Scientific Study of Religion* 47(3):492–502.
Mehta, Sharan Kaur, Rachel C. Schneider, and Elaine Howard Ecklund. 2022. "'God Sees No Color' So Why Should I? How White Christians Produce Divinized Colorblindness." *Sociological Inquiry* 92(2):623–646.
Mikula, Gerold. 1986. "The Experience of Injustice: Toward a Better Understanding of its Phenomenology." Pp. 103–124 in *Justice in Social Relations*, edited by Hans Werner Bierhoff, Ronald Cohen, and Jerald Greenberg. New York: Plenum.
———. 1993. "On the Experience of Injustice." *European Review of Social Psychology* 4(1):223–244.
Miller, Daniel. 2021. "American Christian Nationalism and the Meaning of Religion." *Method and Theory in the Study of Religion* 1:1–22.
Miller, David. 1976. *Social Justice.* Oxford: Oxford University Press.
Miller, Joshua, and Ann Marie Garran. 2007. "The Web of Institutional Racism." *Smith College Studies in Social Work* 77(1):33–67.
Molotch, Harvey. 1972. *Managed Integration: Dilemmas of Doing Good in the City.* Berkeley: University of California Press.
Montada, Leo. 1991. "Coping with Life Stress Injustice and the Question 'Who Is Responsible?'" Pp. 9–39 in *Social Justice in Human Relations*, vol. 2, edited by Herman Steensma and Riel Vermunt. Boston: Springer.
Moore, Wendy. 2008. *Reproducing Racism: White Space, Elite Law Schools, and Racial Inequality.* New York: Rowman and Littlefield.
Moss, Philip, and Chris Tilly. 2003. *Stories Employers Tell: Race, Skill and Hiring in America.* New York: Russell Sage Foundation.

Moule, Jean. 2009. "Understanding Unconscious Bias and Unintentional Racism." *Phi Delta Kappa* 90(5):320–326.

Munn, Christopher W. 2018. "The One Friend Rule: Race and Social Capital in an Interracial Network." *Social Problems* 65(4):473–490.

Neckerman, Kathryn, and Joleen Kirschenman. 1991. "Hiring Strategies, Racial Bias, and Inner-City Workers." *Sociological Review* 60(6):947–65.

Newby, C. Alison, and Julie Dowling. 2007. "Black and Hispanic: The Racial Identification of Afro-Cuban Immigrants in the Southwest." *Sociological Perspectives* 50(3):343–366.

Noy, Chaim. 2008. "Sampling Knowledge: The Hermeneutics of Snowball Sampling in Qualitative Research." *International Journal of Social Research Methodology* 11(4):327–344.

Okuwobi, Oneya Fennell. 2019. "'Everything that I've Done Has Always Been Multiethnic: Biographical Work among Leaders of Multiracial Churches." *Sociology of Religion* 80(4):478–495.

Okuwobi, Oneya, Ruth Powell, and Nicole Ward. 2020. "Ethnic Diversity and Leadership Roles among Australian Protestant Churchgoers in Mono-Ethnic and Multi-Ethnic Congregations." *Research in the Social Scientific Study of Religion* 31:219–250.

Oliver, Melvin, and Thomas Shapiro. 2000. "A Sociology of Wealth and Racial Inequality." Pp. 402–406 in *Readings for Diversity and Social Justice: An Anthology on Racism, Anti-Semitism, Heterosexism, Ableism, and Classism*, edited by Maurianne Adams, Warren Blumenfeld, Rosie Castaneda, Heather Hackman, Madeline Peters, and Ximena Zuniga. New York: Routledge.

Omi, Michael, and Howard Winant. 2015. *Racial Formation in the United States*. 3rd ed. New York: Routledge.

Onwuachi-Willig, Angela. 2017. "Policing the Boundaries of Whiteness: The Tragedy of Being 'Out of Place' from Emmett Till to Trayvon Martin." *Iowa Law Review* 102:1113–1185.

Oyakawa, Michelle. 2019. "Racial Reconciliation as a Suppressive Frame in Evangelical Multiracial Churches." *Sociology of Religion* 80(4):496–517.

Pager, Devah, Bruce Western, and Bart Bonikowski. 2009. "Discrimination in a Low-Wage Labor Market: A Field Experiment." *American Sociological Review* 74(5):777–99.

Parker, James. 1968. "The Interaction of Negroes and Whites in an Integrated Church Setting." *Social Forces* 46(3):359–366.

Prager, Devah, and Diana Karafin. 2009. "Bayesian Bigot? Statistical Discrimination, Stereotypes, and Employer Decision Making." *Annals of the American Academy of Political Science* 621(1):70–93.

Peart, Norman. 2000. *Separate No More: Understanding and Developing Racial Reconciliation in Your Church*. Grand Rapids, Mich.: Baker Book House.

Pérez, Raúl. 2017. "Racism without Hatred? Racist Humor and the Myth of 'Colorblindness.'" *Sociological Perspectives* 60, no. 5: 956–974.

———. 2022. *The Souls of White Jokes: How Racist Humor Fuels White Supremacy*. Stanford, Calif.: Stanford University Press.

Perry, Samuel. 2013. "Religion and Whites' Attitudes toward Interracial Marriage with African Americans, Asians, and Latinos." *Journal for the Scientific Study of Religion* 52:425–442.

Perry, Samuel, and Andrew Whitehead. 2015a. "Christian Nationalism and White Racial Boundaries: Examining Whites' Opposition to Interracial Marriage." *Ethnic and Racial Studies* 38:1671–1689.

———. 2015b. "Christian Nationalism, Racial Separatism, and Family Formation: Attitudes toward Transracial Adoption as a Test Case." *Race and Social Problems* 7:123–124.

Perry, Samuel, Andrew Whitehead, and Joshua Davis. 2019. "God's Country in Black and Blue: How Christian Nationalism Shapes Americans' Views about Police (Mis)treatment of Blacks." *Sociology of Race and Ethnicity* 5(1):130–146.

Pettigrew, Thomas, and Jerome Martin. 1986. "Shaping the Organizational Context for Black American Inclusion." *Journal for Social Issues* 43:41–78.

Pitt, Richard. 2010. "Fear of a Black Pulpit? Real Racial Transcendence Versus Cultural Assimilation in Multiracial Churches." *Journal for the Scientific Study of Religion* 49(2):218–223.

Potenza, Marc. 2013. "Biological Contributions to Addictions in Adolescents and Adults: Prevention, Treatment, and Policy Implications." *Journal of Adolescent Health* 52(2):S22–S32.

Priest, Kersten Bayt, and Robert J. Priest. 2007. "Divergent Worship Practices in the Sunday Morning Hour: Analysis of an 'Interracial' Church Merger Attempt." Pp. 276–293 in *This Side of Heaven: Race, Ethnicity, and Christian Faith*, edited by Robert J. Priest and Alvaro L. Nieves. Oxford: Oxford University Press.

Progress 2050. 2015. "Demographic Growth of People of Color." Center for American Progress, August 2015. https://cdn.americanprogress.org/wp-content/uploads/2015/08/05075256/PeopleOfColor-Democracy-FS.pdf.

Quillian, Lincoln, Devah Pager, Ole Hexel, and Arnfinn H. Midtbøen. "Meta-Analysis of Field Experiments Shows No Change in Racial Discrimination in Hiring over Time." *Proceedings of the National Academy of Sciences* 114(41):10870–10875.

Rahim, Zamira, and Rob Picheta. 2020. "Floyd's Death in Global Display of Solidarity." CNN, June 1. https://www.cnn.com/2020/06/01/world/george-floyd-global-protests-intl/index.html.

Ray, Victor. 2019. "A Theory of Racialized Organizations." *American Sociological Review* 84(1):26–53.

Roach, David. 2020. "Most U.S. Pastors Speak Out in Response to George Floyd's Death." *Christianity Today*, June 16. https://www.christianitytoday.com/news/2020/june/pastors-george-floyd-racism-church-barna-research.html.

Robertson, Campbell. 2018. "A Quiet Exodus: Why Black Worshipers Are Leaving White Evangelical Churches." *New York Times*, March 9. https://www.nytimes.com/2018/03/09/us/blacks-evangelical-churches.html.

Rodriguez, Clara. 2000. *Changing Race: Latinos, the Census, and the History of Ethnicity in the United States*. New York: New York University.

Roediger, David. 1994. *Towards the Abolition of Whiteness: Essays on Race, Politics, and Working Class History*. New York: Verso.

Rogers, Reuel. 2001. "'Black like Who': Afro-Caribbean Immigrants, African Americans and the Politics of Group Identity." Pp. 163–192 in *Islands in the City: West Indian Migration to New York*, edited by Nancy Foner. Berkeley: University of California Press.

Rondilla, Joanne, and Paul Spickard. 2007. *Is Lighter Better? Skin-Tone Discrimination among Asian Americans*. Lanham, Md.: Rowman and Littlefield.

Rowe, Wayne, Sandra Bennett, and Donald Atkinson. 1994. "White Racial Identity Models: A Critique and Alternative Proposal." *Counseling Psychologist* 22:129–146.

Schaffner, Brian, Matthew MacWilliams, and Tatishe Nteta. 2018. "Understanding White Polarization in the 2016 Vote for President: The Sobering Role of Racism and Sexism." *Political Science Quarterly* 133(1):9–34.

Scheitle, Christopher, and Kevin Dougherty. 2010. "Race, Diversity, and Membership Duration in Religious Congregations." *Sociological Inquiry* 80(3):405–423.

Schensul, Stephen, Jean Schensul, and Margaret LeCompte. 1999. *Essential Ethnographic Methods: Observations, Interviews, and Questionnaires*. Walnut Creek, Calif.: AltaMira Press.

Schuman, Howard, Charlotte Steeh, Lawrence Bobo, and Maria Krysan. 1997. *Racial Attitudes in America: Trends and Interpretations*. 2nd ed. Cambridge, Mass.: Harvard University Press.

Sellers, Robert, Mia Smith, J. Nicole Shelton, Stephanie Rowley, and Tabye Chavous. 1998. "Multidimensional Model of Racial Identity: A Reconceptualization of African American Racial Identity." *Personality and Social Psychology Review* 2(1):18–39.

Shelton, Jason E., and M. Nicole Coleman. 2009. "After the Storm: How Race, Class, and Immigration Concerns Influenced Beliefs about the Katrina Evacuees." *Social Science Quarterly* 90, no. 3: 480–496.

Sherkat, Darren, and Derek Lehman. 2018. "Bad Samaritans: Religion and Anti-Immigration and Anti-Muslim Sentiment in the United States." *Social Science Quarterly* 99:1791–1804.

Shortle, Allyson, and Ronald Gaddie. 2015. "Religious Nationalism and Perceptions of Muslims and Islam." *Politics and Religion* 8:435–57.

Smith, Sandra, and Mignon Moore. 2000. "Interracial Diversity and Relations among African-Americans: Closeness among Black Students at a Predominantly White University." *American Journal of Sociology* 106:1–39.

Stewart, Evan. 2018. "Public Religion and the Vote for Donald Trump: Evidence from Panel Data." Paper presented at the American Sociological Association Annual Meeting in Philadelphia.

Stewart, Evan, Penny Edgell, and Jack Delehanty. 2018. "The Politics of Religious Prejudice and Tolerance for Cultural Others." *Sociological Quarterly* 59(1):17–39.

Stoddart, Kellie. 2002. "Researching White Racial Identity: A Methodological Story." *American Behavioral Scientist* 45(8):1254–1264.

Stokes-Brown, Atiya. 2012. "America's Shifting Color Line? Reexamining Determinants of Latino Racial Self-Identification." *Social Science Quarterly* 92(2):309–332.

Stoll, Laurie Cooper. 2014. "Constructing the Color-Blind Classroom: Teachers' Perspectives on Race and Schooling." *Race Ethnicity and Education* 17(5): 688–705.

Szymczak, Wioletta. 2020. "Interdisciplinarity in pastoral theology. An example of socio-theological research." *Verbum Vitae* 38: 503–527.

Tatum, Beverly Daniel. 1993. *Racial Identity Development and Relational Theory: The Case of Black women in White Communities*. Stone Center, Wellesley College.

Taylor, Donald, and Fathali Moghaddam. 1994. *Theories of Intergroup Relations*. New York: Praeger.

Teague, Matthew. 2020. "'He Wears the Armor of God': Evangelicals Hail Trump's Church Photo Op." *Guardian*, June 3, 2020. https://www.theguardian.com/us-news/2020/jun/03/donald-trump-church-photo-op-evangelicals.

Tesler, Michael. 2016. *Post-Racial or Most-Racial*. Chicago: University of Chicago Press.

Thomas, James. 2020. "Diversity Regimes: How University Diversity Initiatives Shape White Race Consciousness." Pp. 71–85 in Lippard, Carter, and Embrick, *Protecting Whiteness*.

Thomas, Jim. 1993. *Doing Critical Ethnography*. Newbury Park, Calif.: Sage.

Tisby, Jemar. 2019. *The Color of Compromise: The Truth about the American Church's Complicity in Racism*. Grand Rapids, Mich.: Zondervan.

Todd, Nathan R., Lisa B. Spanierman, and Mark S. Aber. 2010. "White Students Reflecting on Whiteness: Understanding Emotional Responses." *Journal of Diversity in Higher Education* 3(2):97–110.

Tyler, Tom, and Heather Smith. 1995. "Social Justice and Social Movements." *Institute of Industrial Relations Working Paper* 61:1–86.

Tyler, Tom, Robert Boeckmann, Heather Smith, and Yuen Huo. 1997. *Social Justice in a Diverse Society*. New York: Routledge.

Tynes, Brendesha M., and Suzanne L. Markoe. 2010. "The Role of Color-Blind Racial Attitudes in Reactions to Racial Discrimination on Social Network Sites." *Journal of Diversity in Higher Education* 3(1):1–13.

U.S. Census Bureau. 2013. Retrieved February 8, 2021. "About the Topic of Race." https://www.census.gov/topics/population/race/about.html.

Vaquera, Elizabeth, and Grace Kao. 2006. "The Implications of Choosing 'No Race' on the Salience of Hispanic Identity: How Racial and Ethnic Backgrounds Intersect among Hispanic Adolescents." *Sociological Quarterly* 47(3):375–396.

Vespa, Jonathan, Jamie Lewis and Rosie Kreider. 2013. "America's Families and Living Arrangements: 2012." *U.S. Census Bureau* P20–570. https://www.census.gov/library/publications/2013/demo/p20-570.html.

Virginia General Assembly. 1823. *The Statutes at Large; Being a Collection of All the Laws of Virginia from the First Session of the Legislature, in the Year 1619*, edited by William Hening. New York: R. & W. & G. Bartow.

Wagner, Peter. 1979. *Our Kind of People: The Ethnical Dimensions of Church Growth in America*. Atlanta, Ga.: John Knox Press.

Walster, Elaine, G. William Walster, and Ellen Berscheid. 1978. *Equity: Theory and Research*. Boston: Allyn and Bacon.

Waters, Mary. 1990. *Ethnic Options: Choosing Identities in America*. Berkeley: University of California Press.

———. 1994. "Ethnic and Racial Identities of Second-Generation Black Immigrants in New York City." *International Migration Review* 28(4):795–820.

———. 1999. *Black Identities: West Indian Immigrant Dreams and American Realities*. Cambridge, Mass.: Harvard University Press.

Weffer, Simon, David Embrick, and Silvia Dominguez. 2020. "Colorful Art, White Spaces: How an Art Museum Maintains White Spaces." Pp. 179–193 in Lippard, Carter, and Embrick, *Protecting Whiteness*.

Weine, Stevan, Brandon Kohrt, Pamela Collins, Janice Cooper, Roberto Lewis-Fernandez, Samuel Okpaku and Milton Wainberg. 2020. "Justice for George Floyd and a Reckoning for Global Mental Health." *Global Mental Health* 7(22):1–5.
Weiss, Robert. 1994. *Learning from Strangers: The Art and Method of Qualitative Interview Studies*. New York: Free Press.
Whitehead, Andrew, and Samuel Perry. 2015. "A More Perfect Union? Christian Nationalism and Support for Same-Sex Unions." *Sociological Perspectives* 58:422–440.
———. 2019. "Is a 'Christian America' a More Patriarchal America? Religion, Politics, and Traditionalist Gender Ideology." *Canadian Review of Sociology* 56(2):151–177.
Whitehead, Andrew, L. Landon Schnabel, and Samuel Perry. 2018. "Gun Control in the Crosshairs: Christian Nationalism and Opposition to Stricter Gun Laws." *Socius* 4:1–13.
Williams, Johnny. 2020. "The Unblackening: 'White' License and the 'Nice' Racism Trope." Pp. 43–56 in Lippard, Carter, and Embrick, *Protecting Whiteness*.
Williams, Richard. 1990. *Hierarchal Structures and Social Value: The Creation of Black and Irish Identities in the United States*. Cambridge: Cambridge University Press.
Wimmer, Andreas. 2007. "How (Not) to Think about Ethnicity in Immigrant Societies." *Oxford Centre on Migration, Policy and Society Working Paper Series* 44:7–38.
Wright, Stephen, Donald Taylor, and Fathali Moghaddam. 1990. "Responding to Membership in a Disadvantaged Group: From Acceptance to Collective Protest." *Journal of Personality and Social Psychology* 58(6):994–1003.
Yancey, George. 1999. "An Examination of the Effects of Residential and Church Integration on Racial Attitudes of Whites." *Social Perspectives* 42(2):279–304.
———. 2001. "Racial Attitudes: Differences in Racial Attitudes of People Attending Multiracial and Uniracial Congregations." Pp. 185–206 in *Research in the Social Scientific Study of Religion*, edited by D.L. Moberg and R.L. Piedmont. Leiden, U.K.: Brill.
———. 2003. *One Body, One Spirit: Principles of Successful Multiracial Churches*. Downers Grove, Ill.: Intervarsity Press.
———. 2006. *Interracial Contact and Social Change*. Boulder, Colo.: Lynne Rienner.
Young, Vershawn. 2007. *Your Average Nigga: Performing Race, Literacy, and Masculinity*. Detroit, Mich.: Wayne State.
Zerai, Assata. 2011. "An Assessment of Afro Centrism, Color-Blind Ideology, and Intersectionality." *Race, Gender, and Class* 18(1/2):254–272.

INDEX

affirmative action, 12, 14, 46, 47, 49, 80, 84, 98
Allport, Gordon, 16
Arjannikova, Alexandra, 24

Bernard, Russel H., 120
Black church, 9, 26
Black Lives Matter (BLM), 2–3, 15, 80, 103, 109
Black Racial Identity, 31, 40–42
Black worshipers, 3, 4
Blanchard, Troy, 24
BLM. *See* Black Lives Matter
Blumer, Herbert, 37
Boles, John, 25
Bonilla-Silva, Eduardo, 3–5; on color-blind racism, 46–49, 70, 109–111, 113–114; on honorary Whiteness, 37, 38–40; on style(s) of colorblindness, 63–66; White racial ideology, 8–9, 29–32, 34–35, 111
Brown, Michael, Jr., 3, 103
Brown v. Topeka Board of Education, 10

Castile, Philando, 103
CDA (critical discourse analysis), 124
Christerson, Brad, 25, 29
Cobb, Ryon, 4
Collins, Patricia Hill, 72
color-blind racism, 5, 46, 48–49, 59, 66, 71, 85, 110, 113; abstract, 49–52; cultural racism, 30, 55–60; frames of, 47–49; minimization of racism, 30, 60–62; multiracial congregations and, 29–31; naturalization, 30, 52–55; styles of colorblindness, 63–66; theology and, 79, 81–83, 85

COVID-19 pandemic, 1
critical discourse analysis (CDA), 124
critical ethnography, 122–123

denominations, 8–9
DeYoung, Curtiss, 26
diversity, 28, 90–91; at WWC 91–93
Dominguez, Silvia, 34
Driskill, Gerald, 24
Du Bois, W. E. B., 26, 35

Edwards, Korie L., 5, 24, 27
Embrick, David, 41
Emerson, Michael, 3, 10–11, 24
Evans, Tony, 12

Feagin, Joe, 32, 39
Fine, Gary Alan, 89
Floyd, George, Jr., 1–2, 6, 15, 73–74, 79–80, 82–83, 94, 103–107, 117, 120
Frankenberg, Ruth, 36

Gallagher, Charles, 36
Garner, Eric, 3
German Ideology, The (Marx), 34
Graham, Billy, 10–12
Gray, Freddie, 3, 103

Hardiman, Rita, 37
Hatch, Nathan, 25
Helms, Janet, 36–37
homogenous churches, 25–26
Howard, Judith, 41

143

Index

ideology: in churches, 31; racial, 4, 6, 17, 31, 47–48, 81, 112, 115, 116; racist, 5; reproduction of, 4; White supremacist, 3
institutional racism, 5, 47, 74; macro level, 89; systemic racism, 47, 79

Jim Crow racism, 29
Jones, Robert, 7–10

Kaepernick, Colin, 15, 82–83, 120
Keehn, Molly, 38
King, Martin Luther, Jr., 6, 29, 117

Latinx Racial Identity, 42–43
LeCompte, Margaret, 120
Lee, General Robert E., 13
Lunenburg, Fred, 20

Manis, Andrew, 2
Marti, Gerardo, 26, 31
Martin, Trayvon, 3
Marx, Karl, 34
matrix of domination, 72
McGavran, Donald, 24
Mehta, Sharan Kaur, 31
meso level, 89
Meyer, John, 24
Miller, David, 72
Moore, Wendy Leo, 32
multiracial: churches, 4–6, 17, 21, 24–28, 46, 75, 87, 117; color-blind racism studies, 29–31; complexity of identity, 27; congregations, 16–17, 53, 56, 71–72, 76, 91, 94, 97, 110–112, 115–16; inequality, 28; seven model types, 28

Nationalists. *See* White Christian Nationalism
neo-Confederates. *See* White Christian Nationalism
neo-Nazis. *See* White Christian Nationalism
Noy, Chaim, 121

organizational level, 89
Oyakawa, Michelle, 17

Perkins, John, 12
Perkins, Spencer, 12
police brutality, 1, 6
politicizing racism and justice, 82

racial injustice, 1, 6, 79
racialized organizations, 15, 22, 89–90, 93–97, 112; external sources of, 103–104; legitimate unequal distribution of resources, 96–97; racialization and credentialing, 97–99; racialized decoupling, 99–102; shape agency, 93–96; sources of change in, 102; theory, 93
racial reconciliation, 4, 11–12, 31
racial structures, 33, 89
racism: Jim Crow, 5; religious, 6–7
Ray, Victor, 5, 22, 89–90, 93–104, 109–110, 112–113
Reagan, Ronald, 12
Reconstruction, 9
Rice, Chris, 12
Rice, Tamir, 3, 103
Robertson, Campbell, 2, 3, 4
Roediger, David, 26

schemas, 22, 89–90, 97–98, 114
Schensul, Jean, 120
Schensul, Stephen, 120
Scott, Walter, 3, 103
slavery, 8–9, 12, 24
Smith, Christian, 10–11
social activism, 76, 79, 96, 108–111
social injustice, 73–74
social justice, 11, 17, 22, 30–31, 68, 71–74, 80, 106–107, 112, 116; counterframe, 79, 80–81, 85–86, 112, 115; definition of, 72; response to, 74
social systems theory, 6, 47
socio-theological, 22, 70, 74–77, 114; appeals, 79; color-blind frame, 76–86; minimization of social justice, 76
socio-theologizing of racism, 76
southern evangelicals, 10
southern strategy, 12
Sterling, Alton, 103
St. John's Church, 2
Supreme Court, 3; *Brown v. Topeka Board of Education*, 9
systemic racism. *See* institutional racism

Tarrants, Thomas, 12
Tesler, Michael, 82
theologizing: justice frame, 80; racism as sin, 77–78
Thomas, Jim, 122

uniracial churches, 25–26

Weffer, Simon, 34
White Christian Nationalism, 12–16, 87; definition, 13–14; ideological framework, 14; Unite the Right rally in Charlottesville, Virginia, 13, 15, 82, 103, 120
White Christians, 2, 9, 13; churches and civil rights movement, 10–11; churches of, 7, 21, 25–26; conservative evangelical, 2, 3, 109; evangelical churches of, 3, 4
White homogenous churches, 25–26
White license, 35
Whiteness, 5, 15, 21–22, 24, 32, 35–38, 43, 46, 97, 108, 112; as credential, 90, 98, 107, 113–114; honorary, 38–40, 48
White organizations, 113
White privilege, 33, 35, 57, 61, 98–99
White racial identity, 22, 36–39; models of, 38–39
White racial ideology, 22, 24, 34–36
White space, 21–22, 24, 32–34, 43–44, 49, 91
White supremacist rhetoric, 9
White supremacy, 1, 3, 8–15, 21–22, 29, 32–34, 35, 37, 39, 46, 48
Williams, Johnny, 35
Without Walls Church (WWC), 4, 17–21, 22, 70–72, 111, 119; Administrative Leadership Team (ALT), 20

Yancey, George, 11

Zerai, Assata, 17, 22, 30–31, 109–112, 114; on colorblindness, 70–72, on theologizing justice frame, 80, 84–87, 109–112, 114

www.ingramcontent.com/pod-product-compliance
Lightning Source LLC
Chambersburg PA
CBHW020936230426
43666CB00008B/1694